CW01425733

The Movement to Love

By Samantha Chappell

Foreward

My calling to write this book came from my life experiences. As my life continued to unveil, I began to realise how empathetic in my nature I was to the world and everyone around me, that I was attempting to save people (as most people in the world do) from things, other people, even sometimes from themselves- anything I thought would harm them. I found myself extremely weighed down by life overall. Through my upbringing I was nurtured into Catholicism attending a catholic primary school and high school. After life's ordeals of relationship break downs, family drama, struggling with destructive behaviours- as all teenagers do- I began to reflect on my life circumstances and what was being mirrored back to me. As my career profession is being an Early Childhood Teacher, I was faced with the knowledge of how detrimental your childhood upbringing can be in an individual's psychological mind. In conjunction with this knowledge I am able to understand the importance of constant reflection- due to the requirements placed on students to attain their bachelor degrees, and even teachers for their on-going professional development. From my knowledge I was able to backtrack where any childhood traumas in my life had been projected into my reality today.

That was only the beginning.

The next step was to either continue onwards in the direction I was heading in, to which I found meant I would keep manifesting and encountering the exact same situations and pain, until I learnt- or I could change and stop using materialistic objects to suppress the need to heal. Then came the decision to change. So instead of repeating a life where I knew the lessons but could not be bothered with the healing process, I began to an endeavour to heal.

Reverting back to how I was brought up in my childhood, I started to go to church on a Sunday again, until I still felt a yearning inside for some deeper kind of truth that I had no idea about what I was searching for. Until my friend told me to read this book *'The Power of Now'* by Eckhart Tolle. I read this book and it was exactly what I needed and it completely changed my mindset. This was until I went on a holiday and after coming back from this euphoric holiday (freedom feeling), I cried to my mum telling her how stupid it was that we have to pay for mud and bricks, fruit and vegetables, and we call this a life- whereby she replied with a blank look of "yes this is reality, welcome to my life". But since then I had this urge inside of me to evolve more, learn more, just find my truth of why I am here on this planet at this exact moment consciously.

I then started my career as a teacher and began observing the education system, other teachers, myself and how humans learnt and were trained in general. After this, I wanted no part in this system, I thought seriously and worked hard at starting a clothing label with my sister and becoming a singer, until I realised each of these weren't for me. A friend told me about how meditation changed their life and before this I always associated meditation with praying, and a negative correlation between the two acts. Although I can now confidently advocate for anyone to meditate, wherever and whoever you are. But from this spark of curiosity, I started a spiritual voyage of not just travelling to see the world but travelling within to see my world and I thank so many spiritual teachers, yogis, genuinely kind people I have met- because through all of this I found a truth, my truth and the truth for all and that is loving unconditionally.

Although one spiritual teacher told me "sometimes you are insecure that you have a sensitive heart, but this is actually your greatest strength". So indeed I have a sensitive heart, but I think if I can share this with the world and help others find their strengths- as everyone has a heart- we can all realise our own potentials and become aware of how beautiful this world is. We are all here at the exact same time, all coming back to remember how to unconditionally love, what is a more beautiful connection than this.

The focus of the book is based on making you aware of the structure of information processing. The main relation is in regards to *'Herman Hollerith's tabulating machine'²*, whereby I attempt to write on how the structure can be evidently reflected on each of the systems today.

The idea of Ivan Pavlov's experiment is how I grasped Skinner's *'operant conditioning'⁷* and respondent behaviour theory. Pavlov conducted an experiment where he discovered that when ringing a bell he gave a dog (the participant) a treat, each time he rang the bell- over the course of the experiment- the dogs mouth would salivate (drool) and would receive a treat. He then rang the bell and without giving the dog a treat, the dogs mouth still salivated automatically- relating the bell to receiving the treat, even when there was no treat. This is the foundation of the classical conditioning and identifying the unconditioned (biological response) of ringing the bell and getting a treat. This salivation he found as a biological response to the previous events of the treat being brought together with the bell. The behaviour was unconditioned as the dog's biological process, following the dog salivating each time, the bell was rung with no evident treat. Although within this book Skinner is the main behaviourist I refer to, though I intended on adapting the experiment Pavlov conducted into Skinner's theory. As Skinner encompassed the effects of both the positive and negative reinforcers, and how the individual voluntarily responds from their conditioning. The result of the *'operant conditioning'⁷* (also known as the *classical conditioning*) assists on explaining how a humans basic needs are conditioned primarily into a being, and how one subconsciously reacts on them when they are not fulfilled. Skinner's theory is essential within this book, as it provides the knowledge of how human's behave. This knowledge gives you the basis of how to become aware of your voluntary actions (*respondent behaviour*), from your classically conditioned (*operant conditioned*) state.

I also refer to the spiritual teacher Eckhart Tolle who helps further the analysis of the inferior and superior egoic conditioned mind, when remarking the *'pain-body'¹*. He describes the *'pain-body'¹* as: *'a negative energy field that occupies your body and mind'* [1] This type of negative energy I embrace to portray the image of how the emotions are merely an energetic force in motion, which can

[1] Tolle, E. (2004), p.36.

be trapped inside your being when you are not aware of the force behind such a frequency.

More recently a friend had guided me to read *'The Divine Matrix'* by Gregg Braden. I had listened to one of his interviews before this on the Youtube and am currently up to page four, and I can already- logically- reinforce what I had written on paper about the matrix of reality, from his studies in the quantum area. From what I'd seen from my meditative state and the channeling of this book, I can now give thanks to those who have walked this path before me also in their works. Through a quantum perspective he states; *'The Divine Matrix is the container that holds the universe, the bridge between all things, and the mirror that shows us what we have created' (p.4).* In the matrix that I refer to I am referring to the current construct of the corporate world, as this is the constructed grid that has been manifested in today's society.

The main concepts I portray to you in this book are those I've witnessed in my own evolution and have been able to understand and see through personal meditation.

I write of the third dimension, where I am referring to the reality which you are brought up in. I reflect on the classic Western Society of corporations ruling the imperialist dimension. This I attempt to portray to you through an explanation of the system structures today and how you are being 'spoon-fed' (programmed) information.

The higher dimension I speak of is that of the fifth dimension where you are connected with your soul (life purpose), hence you are in alignment with the Universe (God), and can draw connections to other beings, through respecting their soul missions.
In between these dimensions is the fourth dimension where you have a connection with the fifth dimension of your soul purpose and implement it into the third dimension of the corporate world, the industrial world.

Embracing these notions of the dimensions, this book is laid out to awaken you to your soul purpose. This is embraced in the book through chapter I. The Pursuit of Evolution, II. The Catastrophe of the Conditioned Mind, and III. The Subtle War on

Information; as they are all directly linking you to awaken to the third dimensional construct and how is it directly linked with your 'being' today. The chapters IV. The Channelings of the Soul, and V. The Movement to Love, relate to the fifth dimension of the universal order. The chapters VI. The Tool of Vulnerability, VII. The Emotional Landscape, VIII. The Polarity of Balancing Energies, and IX. The Return to the Unconditional; All relate to how to bring in the purpose of your soul to fruition, hence the fourth dimension of becoming aware of understanding the need to ground down into your heart space.

Chapters

- I. The Pursuit of Evolution.
- II. The Catastrophe of the Conditioned Mind.
- III. The Subtle War on Information.
- IV. The Channelings of the Soul.
- V. The Movement to Love.
- VI. The Tool of Vulnerability.
- VII. The Emotional Landscape.
- VIII. The Polarity of Balancing Energies.
- IX. The Return to the Unconditional.

I.   The Pursuit of Evolution.

When you are born it appears you enter the world through a portal. A particular body has been given to you, with a certain set number of ligaments, DNA, bones, muscles, organs, pigments on your skin all constructed in a particular way. The make-up and binding of atoms and molecules together in a particular shape and form come together to house your soul. You appear to be here for a certain period of time, meeting a certain number of people, to learn particular lessons. Your mind is metaphorically on fire and you are ready to learn, asking questions, learning to speak, learning to walk, sit, stand, eat with teeth, share, interact with others. Your mind is a vessel picking up oxygen (information) wherever it can in order to fit into this new place (Earth) as quickly as it can, in order to survive and fulfil your soul mission. Which in retrospect is a complete conscious paradox to your being as you have no conscious knowledge of where you're heading, but you have a drive to achieve independence, in order to complete your evolutionary mission.

The overall outcome of your mission is that your soul is here for an evolutionary purpose, as Earth is a basis for our learning. The hardship which your soul encounters through this entails obstacles and events to test your learning (your evolution) and further your oneness with your evolutionary success. This drives the basis of your pursuit of your evolution- the subconscious need for love and oneness. Your evolutionary process I will attempt to portray in a metaphorical sense. As your evolutionary process continues you begin to encounter closed doors, which have a key. Paradoxically, the key often finds its way to you, instead of your endless searching for this key. You have a yearning to do something, an intuitive motive subconsciously, a present moment gift, spur-of-the-moment idea where you reach towards something and go for that... All of a sudden behind this locked door there is a room with a chair in the corner, and with each experience there is a bell ringing without your 'being' able to hear it. You sit on the chair subconsciously, and here it comes, an event, a certain amount of people, certain songs, certain words, certain sceneries, play and play. And you are still in the corner. You watch; you watch it all unfold and then you join in, you're in the midst of the chaos of love, lust, happiness, sadness, anger, guilt, heartache, pain and betrayal and then it all disappears and you sit on the chair again.

Words written on the walls, songs playing dedicated to the event to remind your being of your emotions. Number sequences, of dates and times, to remind you of the event in different ways. The colours flash of the emotions on the wall and your chair spins round and round. And it stops. Silence. Peace.

You're still on the chair sitting and a tear falls down for your conscious mind believed the chaos was a little fuller, for your survival technique is to stand in the crowd and feel at one.

Just as you stop your tears, it happens again. The bell ringing in blind sight, so you don't realise and you watch a new event unfold before you, the scene, the characters, the lines, the emotions, and you find yourself off your chair and attached again. You talk, you live, you cry, you laugh, you show anger, you experience it all. When just in that moment you realise it's beautiful, it all disappears again and you sit back on the chair and you wonder why, why it happened, where it all went, analysing these new emotions you've been gifted inside. When it all happens again the room is covered in words, the room echoing songs, the lights flashing colours of what you feel inside, the chair spinning in a certain amount of degrees and you sit on the chair and release the energy built up from the events and embrace all the stained markings found on the walls and the room, like a heavy cloud until it all stops again. You begin to smile, the light has turned white, the walls all white, the speakers turned off, your chair back in the corner. Then the bell rings again—you're taken on the same journey, it stops and your chair pushes towards the middle of the room, and the tainted markings of the emotional event starts again.
This time you scream and shout instead of the tears and you resist all your emotions inside. It stops but from your past experiences you carry each manifested emotional conclusions into the next event and the next event and the next event, until your 'being' begins to get accustomed to the ordeals. Each time you've gained a vivid memory of the pains before.

Until to your surprise, one event shows you a glimpse of the key, this key is in a glass box with a lock reading a riddle. This event gives you a glimpse of before you were born, the feelings of the divine, the eternal and you're happy, you're at peace. It then leaves, and the event encloses and vanishes and you're back on your chair. The riddle puzzles you but the light is still on, the walls are not written on nor speaking aloud, and you know it's a truth to open the door but you don't quite know what the riddle means or what's behind the door, but you're entrapped in an intuitive drive to move towards it. Thinking how, and what it means, you realise the only way to open the glass box is to solve the riddle and ultimately open the door to what you believe is life.

The next event that unfolds you go into It questioning, searching, asking the characters. You embrace it all, although after the event absolute chaos unfolds, lights are flashing, walls are beaming, a voice is playing over lines of the characters and your chair spins and rotates around. It stops and you feel a sudden break but you become hostile in the riddle, in the pursuit. You wonder why you're so hostile, so angry that it beats you up more, infinite circles and events to remind you and challenge the anger that you've built up inside from this subconscious yearning for that infinite peaceful feeling. Your body moving in and out of events, your mind a subject of your uncertainty, of your search for the key and hence the door being unlocked to the next adventure.

After experiencing immense amounts of events, you're sitting on the chair, where you have gained wisdom from these events and you've realised your patterns, the egotistical drive of feeding your addictive nature of urgency. A demanding lifestyle to which you had witnessed and succumbed to over and over again. So you await, breathe, find the peace of yourself in the chaos, and once again the bell rings. You knew consciously now it was coming and you are thrown into the situation, an event, labelling is forgotten and you just pass through it, you're grounded and knew that despite it all, you had yourself. Getting so accustomed to the light inside you, you begin to tell the other characters of the light, but they're reciting what they have been conditioned to know, nodding to your string of light and in contrast subconsciously making you into the problem. You go back into your chair and it fades, the walls taunting you deeper now, the light fading black, the speakers over and over, but you sit on your chair, for a second you question yourself, you then breathe and find peace in it all. You realise the love of your evolution and being, knowing it was bigger than it all, and within this the taunting stops. Your chair in the middle of the room now. You're sitting down still and an event unfolds in front of you. This event is your hardest one yet and unknown to your conscious knowledge your last event. There's the world in that event and you look each individual character in the eyes and you see yourself, a piece of you from sometime ago or now or in the future, and you send them your love. Without the key or the riddle, the door opens by itself, you're not shocked but you're ready, you knew it was the goal all along but you stay to thank the room and chair for giving you this opportunity and then you leave through the door.

This is life.
Your pursuit of your evolution.
The room is your mind.
The chair is your physical vessel.
The events your obstacles.
The door your return to the cycle of evolution.
You, the universal energy.

So why is the pursuit of your evolution so important?
Well it's the introduction into expanding your awareness, of returning to home. The only way to change the events, is no way. To change your reactions is to change yourself and evolve. The only way to change yourself is to acknowledge that you, and only you, holds the power to do this all along. You are in control of yourself, you are you- A unique individual made up of a particular amount of atoms and molecules all placed together to house the universal energy that inadvertently holds us altogether, makes us all the same and provides us all with an ultimate goal which we each strive for. The pursuit of evolving is not to be caught up in one egoistic truth of 'zen' in the fifth dimension or a religion of "one truth". Nor is evolving to be caught up in a truth of societal achievements, money currency or politics, all in the third dimension, but rather allowing your being to come to Earth to evolve in such a way, that it will encounter events placed there by the universe to test you on your own evolution.

Perhaps, as written on the room of the tauntings (the above introduction) or events, that there will be an outside "conditioning" either consciously or subconsciously whereby your soul is dimmed if you allow it or brightened if you allow it. Although there will be external factors to which you decide to haunt you, until you learn your lessons for your evolution, or evolve forward. The chair is akin to your body, it will enable your soul to get by and do the things in order for you- the universal energy- to be grounded and evolutionise. Which means if you allow your mind to succumb to the event, your body will also spin you round and round with the rollercoaster of life. Your events are your obstacles- they can be the 'best' and the 'worst' all at once for your being, depending on the way you have faith in the pursuit of your evolution. The door and any taste of the door subconsciously drives you, depending on how you look at it ultimately determines your mind state. Although in regards to this mind state all your connections to any character (person) you encounter in life, has a common goal and ultimately you have something in common with every single one of them, which unites us all.

You- the universal energy- you are the power. The power in all of this. You came to Earth for a reason, every single encounter is for your evolution, because you are eternal. You can look in your own eyes and just become aware there's someone beautiful. For the love in your heart, for the cries in a baby, for the darkness in adolescence, for the happiness in a family, it's all coming home to love.

It's all the same needs and desires, there's nothing more reassuring than the love in your heart, for when you connect with another individual, looking truly into someone's eyes lets you see their soul. When another being is talking or crying or giving a smile to a 'stranger', there's love. There's love all around for you and for the universe. There's nothing greater or lesser, just love.

When you're a child you listen to what your parents have to say, you take in all the information you can receive. You discover as much as you can, observing and attempting to help family members, carers, teachers, friends, all to learn as much as you can and seize the moment. As you grow up, you begin to question why it is the way things are. Learning about your life more and more, not to mention extra hormones driving your physical and mental being more than ever before. You begin to have a voice, 'finding' your feet, attempting to find a 'truth' and stick by it to make it in a third dimensional matriarchal system. You begin to question the ones around you on why they demand authority over you, challenging their beliefs of how you should be and you challenging theirs on why it should or should not be a certain way.

Children are the creative beings, the purest gifts to this world, naturally imbued with the universal energy, in order to fit into this world, not realising they evolve into someone else's desires or dreams. They conform to feel wanted in a place unknown to them and as they grow up and subconsciously feel a sense of belonging they convert subconsciously to awaken out of their old self. They are now transitioning and 'discovering' what they need in order to evolutionise, this could go on for years and years until they return home to themselves and realise that it's all for the process of evolution. You could filter it with any addictive, egotistical behaviour which is seen, or you could forgive your being with your own love in your heart and know you never had the plan or control.

You are you, her, him, it, you are it all- as it's all connected to the universal energy, and yet- you are you, also individually. There was a subconscious, innate necessity a yearning inside to experience through a certain event, in order to develop and evolutionise. It was all necessary and all illusory and for your highest good most importantly. You begin to own your scars and know how to evolutionise further to vibrate empathy into the universe and return home. You realise it's not being in one truth, one soul truth, there's no other truth than the love for your being. Once you love your being, you know what to lead with, in order to lead by example. Not with your words of the mind. But with the soul of your heart. That's the true coming home to your being and your soul mission.

So what even is your being you may ask?
Overall it is the physical, mental and spiritual combination that is you. Placed on this earth, in this certain amount of particular molecules and atoms to make-up your systematic functioning in this three dimensional, certain period of time.

So what is the pursuit?
Everyone has some sort of goal or certain subconscious drive that motivates them as we all have one thing in common, that stands out... We will all die in the physical body one day. Despite different beliefs of the afterlife, where will we go once passing out of this third dimensional grounded being? One thing is for certain- we will pass out of this human body, which everyone is aware of. In retrospect is does bring people together at certain times of need around the world and close to home. But this one common acknowledgement of how life is and will come about, can drive the human race and yourself. Maybe you'd never thought about it before, or maybe you had but hadn't alchemised it to empower yourself to your fullest potential. But this notion of death is your driving force, your pursuit of evolution, whether you knew this subconsciously or consciously.

So what is your evolution or what is evolution?

Whatever happens, happens.

Such is life.

Cést la vie.

Your evolution is in those days where you look back and realise every single choice, encounter, experience was all linked after all. It was all necessary for this growing. This growing of the soul that tells you, "yes this is exactly what I needed". Those events that used to boil your emotions or maybe they still do boil your emotions, those times you wanted to give up and one little small voice inside said to keep going. In this is your evolution. The universe never said it was easy, or God, or anyone, but it was all necessary and is necessary for you to one day look back and know why each event happened as it did, as it led you to the individual- yet whole-hearted person you are now. That is your evolution. That's where you ground-break, and fly all at the same time.

II.   The Catastrophe of the Conditioned Mind.

This chapter is broken up into three sections of the dimensions in order to further your awareness on your life purpose.

Part One: The third dimensional construct in society today:
The catastrophe of the conditioned mind can be best put into context through one man's machine. This machine can be seen everywhere in this three-dimensional 'reality'. If you look around right now wherever you are I am sure you can either see a mobile phone or a computer of some sort- That is the evolution of his machine to your knowing eye (at this point). This evolution of his machine goes further in the third dimensional construct in today's society through the categorisation of a living being.
Allow me to explain.

The theory is as follows.
Who?
A man named Herman Hollerith (*'b. Feb. 29, 1860, Buffalo, N.Y., US'*[2]) created a *tabulating machine* for the 1890 census in the United States. In reference to *The New Encylopaedia Britannica 'he had invented machines to record statistics by electrically reading and sorting punched cards that had been numerically encoded by perforation position'*[2].

The original aim?
His invention mainly consisted of the aim to process large amounts of information electrically. For quicker processing of information.

The eventuated aim?
To sort individuals into overall mass categories, through processing and sorting.

What is a tabulating machine?
The machine works on an electric current where when one piece of paper was assigned to an individual, the operator could look at the information received from the census survey and place a hole in a certain spot on the card, to

---

[2] Encylopaedia Britannica. (2005). *The New Encylopaedia Britannica, Volume 6.* U.S.A: Encylopaedia Britannica Inc.

correspond to a certain trait (of the participant) for easier sorting and categorising of information when analysing the overall country.

How is this put into practice?
As an example; A survey may ask if you are a farmer or not? Human one (called Bill) is a farmer and human two (called Bob) is not a farmer. The operator will get this information from the survey. The operator will have instructions on punching the paper. Instructions consist of the left side of the paper indicating a 'no'. The instructions consist of the right side of the paper indicating 'yes'. The operator writes the names on the pieces of the paper. The operator places Bill's paper into the tabulating machine and punches a hole in the right side of the paper. The operator takes out Bill's piece of paper to indicate 'yes'. The operator places Bob's paper into the tabulating machine and punches a hole in the left side of the paper to indicate 'no'. It then allowed the operators and those concerned to analyse and categorise the information from the survey electrically without having to sort through each individual survey and the results.

How did it progress?
Hollerith later created an automatic feeder which by automation from electricity allowed the operators job to vanish. The operator's job was now to correct any errors that the automatic feeder made through mishaps, by checking over the papers after it had been punched in the machine.

What he had to say about this.
He stated: *'My idea was to use a strip of paper and punch the record for each individual in a line across the strip. Then I ran this strip over a drum and made [electrical] contacts through the hole to operate the counters. This, you see, gave me the idea of an ideal automatic feed'.* He used his designs to assist the collection of the 1890 census for the United States which the government officials could analyse: *'Various statistical items for a given person,"* Hollerith explained, *"are recorded by punching suitable holes in a line across the strip, being guided by letters on the guide plate"* (a template superimposed over the tape). *The position of the hole indicated whether a person was male or female, native or foreign-born, and white or colored, in addition to his or her age category. Once the record was made, the strip was advanced over rollers to repeat the operation. Hollerith verified the individual portraits by placing a lettered template, similar to the guide plate, across the paper strip. Small seals of*

paper were used to cover wrongly punched holes'[3].

What eventuated further?
An automatic *'sorting box'[3]* designed to arrange the information recorded into the designed desired categories that the survey creator wanted to find out from the survey.

How was this used?
In reference to Austrian (1982): *'The lid of a particular box popped open when a card with certain characteristics- say, white females- was sensed by the circuit-closing press'.* Austrian (1982) wrote how *'War Departments', 'Navy Department', 'Department's records and Pension Division',* all began using this tabulating machine and sorting box for their collections of *'sick reports'[3]* and individual classifications and overall whole group classifications.

What eventuated next?
Hollerith added on to his tabulating machine and sorting box by adding a *'semi-automatic', 'pin-box mechanism'[3]* where he added electricity to have: *'An electric motor under the desk-top work surface of the tabulator closed the plate upon the pin box and then moved it away to allow for the insertion and sensing of the next card'[3].* He explained how; *'The fingers fall as the plate recedes, allowing the card to drop into the receiving box below'[3].*

The issue he found..
'But if the card is defective or has been carelessly inserted, no tabulation occurs, and the fingers retain the card'[3]. Making a restriction of how individuals information is processed in the system, as the system falls short. The tabulation makes it as if there is a grid system of how the ideal individual will fit into the system (analysed on punched holes and non-punched holes) due to the system creators desired outcomes.

What eventuated next?
Then in *'1902'[3]: 'The latest development of the Hollerith system is the automatic machine in which the work of separately placing each card beneath the pin box,*

---

[3] Austrian, G.D. (1982). *Forgotten Giant of Information Processing.* USA: Columbia University Press.

depressing the pin box, and removing the card is performed automatically...
instead of by hand'[3].

How was the machine put into practice?
From the information received, the card is placed into the machine through automation. The machine senses the information received and converts this information to place a hole in a specific place on the piece of paper to indicate a certain piece of information. The card is then placed into a sorting box of specific categories, in correspondence to the punched hole from the information received. The machine then automatically receives the next card and continues the process.

So why is this analogy necessary in explaining the concept of the conditioned mind, today?
In summary, Herman Hollerith created a machine designed to easily record information more quickly and more simply originally for the government census. This notion of information processing can be seen in pretty much any system we have in place today.

His machine in practice today?
The categorisation of an individual being consists within the systems today such as the health care systems, the education systems and evidently the structure of the corporate world.

The positive outlook of this machines practice in today's society?
It puts in place a system that is designed to quickly record information on an individual, in order to progress the individuals needs and desires.

The negative outlook of this machines practice in today's society?
It puts in place a system that is designed to quickly record information on an individual, in order to analyse their previous information to statistically market them to the corporate world.
As a basic example: Bill often banks money on his phone on a Monday. Each Monday companies send Bill an email to market to Bill they are having a sale. The assumption made is Bill's data of banking on Mondays has been recorded and corporations now know what day Bill is likely to succumb to his needs and desires. Corporations are using Bill's previously recorded information as a catalyst

for their corporate gains.

Another example: Bill often complains of a back pain to his physiotherapist. The physiotherapist has often worked on Bill's back pain with his physical hands. Bill sees a doctor for his back pain, Bill believes he is tired of his back pain and there are no alternatives. The doctor analyses him and from his observations the doctor is able to market Bill a product that he believes cures back pain.

How is the machine in practice in regards to the systems?

As an example as soon as you arrive on earth your given name is established and placed on a card (a birth certificate) with your given name, names of your family members, your place of birth, physical gender, mother, father, mother's societal status and background information, father's societal status and background information: these are all recorded.

Another example is the health care system as it categorises your health of the physical body and mental mind based upon observations of trials and errors. Such as the recordings of previous information of names given, dates, mental illnesses or damage, immunisations, medications, allergies, intolerances and physical illnesses or damage.

Another example is the educational system. Where during the years of your education whether that be attending early childhood settings, primary school, high school or university, they intend to collect as much data about you, in order to categorise your physical and mental capabilities. The educational systems intend on sorting the data that is collected about you, in order to know how to further advance your capabilities. The aim is seen as advancing your capabilities by training your mind with as much information, on as many different topics, as you can take, and test you on how much information you can retain. They then can further categorise your abilities to reflect the system in which they have in place and intend to best manipulate it to help the individuals.

The negative aspect to the educational system is when the system can fall short and base their advancement of an individual's capabilities to reflect their corporate price on how well you can perform and their overall average, in comparison to other educational corporations. This further builds a hierarchy of educational corporations through comparison of retained information.

The positive aspect to the educational system is that now you are given the information to function in the third dimensional construct of reality, you can then educate yourself with the tools you have attained.

Within the working field you are directed into a corporate construct of the world. This construct is based upon a capitalist mentality.

This is an example of the negative side of the corporate world: Bill attends a job meeting where a panel judges his capabilities. The panel tells Bill that based upon your profile as an individual, 'we will assess you to see if you are applicable to sell your life hours for our capitalist benefits. If you get chosen you will be given a reward of a decimal point sum (money), so that you can feel as if you're an important member of something and valued for processing your information of our companies needs'.

The following is an example of the positive side of the corporate world: Bill feels as if he is satisfied within himself based on the information he has retained and the respect of the construct of information in his mind that society has given him from this. Bill feels important. Bill is at peace with the workings of his mind and thus is not feeling the negativity of giving his time away. Bill feels he has contributed to helping society.

So what is all this about? What does it mean? How is it applicable to you?

Well I believe that if you change yourself you can change the world, and if in some way I can help you see how the world works and alchemise the situation of your mindset, I know you can contribute to this world effectively.

Every system today is theoretically based upon on a computer system, and this guy (Herman Hollerith) paved the way for this movement (unintentionally) and just like anything in this world there is a positive and a negative to it. He himself noted how it was only for processing large amounts of information, not people. The aim of the machine was designed to make it easier for large companies to make a collection of data from the past. Although in this society it is hard to break the chain of conforming to the processing of information as we live in a processed world, where people risk their lives at points to get the best videos of themselves, to share on online forums. We live in a society which is run by technology, conforming to the minds of a processing forum, forgetting to use not only our creative minds, but also our logical minds to the best of its abilities. Forgetting our whole brains, left and right sides, as we hand it over to corporations to fill our brains in for us.

We live in a society of the ego, a society of comparison, a society as Gregg Braden best described it as, *'competition, conflict, struggle and scarcity'* [4] .

---

[4] *Morgan Arts Council, 2018.*

We live in a society ran by our conditioned minds, our reptilian brain where we feed our pain with external factors and then make others the problem, never reflecting on our own skeletons in the closet, and completely forgetting our own personal power, our own evolutionary process, and the one thing that is holding us altogether, which is unconditional love. This one subconscious fear of knowing one day we will die in this physical body, and this fear of the unknown afterwards, drives our emotions and minds, rather than igniting our souls. We begin to panic, about time, the third dimension of reality that we've lost contact with all our senses. Our gentle nature, our inner child, our wisdom, our connection to the planets and each other, but mainly ourselves. We are so consumed by processing ourselves to conform day in day out (so we aren't an error in the system) that we wake up to our devices to check social forums on what everyone else is doing, and comparing ourselves to a snippet of one's reality, that we've lost complete sight of our own power. Our own inner wisdom, guidance and the intuitive sense that we are here for a purpose. Haven't you ever asked yourself or muttered- "I know there's got to be more to life"?

There certainly is when you change your perspective. When you change yourself, you are allowing your own vibrational frequency to change and hence attracting a new frequency that matches your frequency into your life. Every single encounter you have manifested in this certain life is for a particular reason, to learn a particular lesson about yourself. So before you go shouting "why is this happening to me?", "why are these events occurring?", "what is wrong with society?" .
Take a breath.
Learn the lesson for your own self.
Then proceed.

The conditioned mind is based upon a three dimensional matrix of the reptilian mind; our yearning for basic needs. Deeply reflected in Gregg Braden's views of, *'competition, conflict, struggle and scarcity'*[4]. These are the notions that reinforces and feeds your mind to believe everything is an opponent on this earth. It reinforces the analysis of examining every single possible external factor, forcing your thinking patterns to go on an infinite loop so you are a 'productive member' in society's eyes and are steered away from actually revealing the infinite power of you. It is your time to become aware that you are a free evolutionary member of the universe. It's time to embrace the paradox that it's all important and an essential process in your evolution. So you have a choice of going through selling hours of your life away for a decimal point currency at the end of each week- you receive, and spend it on items which you believe aren't free (that are given to us from nature). But in saying all this one day, 'when it's all said and done', you begin to realise it was all necessary and you revert back to love, love for your own being and hence the world.

Nothing is more whole.

Nothing more worthy.

Paradoxically everything is whole and worthy at the exact same judgement- and yet in regards to this notion -if you realise your own: evolution, love and abundance within yourself; you can then connect with the everlasting notion of your own being. Just as the moon and the sun are equivalently beneficial and essential when compared to each other, so are your perceived judgements of the negative and positive events in your life.

Part Two: The fourth dimensional construct in society today:
The fourth dimensional construct in society today I will attempt to explain the construction through 'psychologists' and 'behaviourists' in history.

'The existence of an organised totality which is preserved while assimilating the external world raises, in effect, the whole problem of life itself. But, as the higher cannot be reduced to the lower without adding something, biology will not succeed in clarifying the question of assimilation without taking into account its psychological aspect. At a certain level life organization and mental organization only constitute, in effect, one and the same thing'[5] — Jean Piaget.

In theory the stages through- age- can assist in recognising the theory. When you are a child you are subjected to endless teachings from different perspectives (parents, teachers, friends, family, community): you are then conforming to what you hear or learn from these perspectives. You find out how to fit into a world completely unknown to you in this third dimension, becoming grounded into the matriarchal system. Becoming conditioned to the societal aspects of the particular culture. John Bowlby describes the exploration in a child's nature in his _'Attachment and Loss'_ book where he observed a child: _'At first something wholly strange elicits only withdrawal. Next comes inspection from a distance- often intense and prolonged. Then, sooner or later, provided the object remains stationary and emits no startling sounds or sights, the object is likely to be approached and explored—at first cautiously, later with more confidence. In most creatures such a process is greatly speeded up in the presence of a friend; and in a young creature especially it is notably accelerated by the presence of mother'[6]._

So this is the way in which each child survives and even you survive in unknown environments. Not to mention early childcare centres or having an absent mother or father, it depletes the ease of trust in the discovery of unknown environments (such as, the earth). This is the foundation of the natural (nature) objective also working with the nurture objective. As you have this physical side of the notion whereby this is the essence of how one survives and thrives in an unfamiliar environment, we then move on to the focus of the unfamiliar environment. As the child- maybe it's even your inner child so you can relate to this notion

---

[5] Piaget, J. (1953), p.46.
[6] Bowlby, J. (1982), p.239.

empathetically in your life—becomes comfortable through seeking the assistance of a naturally trusted 'superior' individual, we can then existentially relate this to the control system which we are conforming to today.

The behaviour of your 'being' stems from the conditioned patterns of your childhood upbringing. If you watch a child evolve, you can observe evidently the patterns which they go through to trust the earth. If for some reason a child is subjected to an event, to which they label as traumatic, no matter how intense they will begin to attach an emotion to these certain events.

If you close your eyes and imagine the very first time you became angry, allow your mind to pinpoint exactly how old you were and what occurred, this is the notion of attaching emotions (energy) to certain events and to your inner child.

'Some trouble no doubt arises from the fact that human behaviour is a sensitive field'. –B.F. Skinner 1974[7].

Your *'human behaviour'*[7] is such a *'sensitive field'*[7] as I will explain further why here and shed some light on how paradoxically without your knowledge your ego will either:
1) Turn it around and you will do the opposite behaviour subconsciously of what you have read.
2) Do the extreme of the behaviour you have read.

Both are extremes of the ego:
1) Confident ego.
2) Not so confident ego.

In behaviourism and psychology they call this:
1) Superior ego; finding yourself more superior from the knowledge you have retained.
2) Inferior ego; finding yourself with a lack of confidence either due to fear inside your body from the knowledge you have retained or a lack of retaining information.

Don't be too hard on yourself, remind yourself it's completely necessary for your evolution to recognise these patterns.
So you can relate this to either yourself or human behaviour in others, if you're not at the awareness of recognising your own mind-set and hence not at the transforming stage in your evolution. Both are completely fine and necessary in your evolution. There are no levels in life, no comparisons, remember you are you. Time is a completely made up construct of the human conditioned mind in an attempt to make sense of something nonsensical (the universe). When observing the timelines of the world your awareness can be brought back to the knowledge that we are all this the 'present time space', yet according to the third dimensional construct of 'reality' there is different times in the world. As an example: One could be in Australia and it could be 1200 hours and one could be in Canada and it could be 2200 hours the day before, yet we are all

---

[7] Skinner, B.F. (1974), p.7-46.

simultaneously living the same moments. Another example of the construct of the third dimensional matrix is the speed of light. As not even the accuracy of the speed of light exists, as scientists collated an approximation from the different recordings from around the world, as they found the speed of light ever changing and incapable of measuring with the observed human mind.

Back onto topic...
The control system, the matrix, the matriarchal society in which you find yourself in today (in this third dimension) can be seen through a capitalist society whereby you are in a reward system for your efforts of contributing to this system.
Let me explain.
All throughout your 'lifespan' in the third dimension you are given an expectation, once you meet this expectation you are given a reward (of materialism- currency) where you are subconsciously trained to be a subject of this system and contribute to this system.

As an example...
Hopefully it's relatable and you can extend in your own minds from there...

A Human...
As a child you are enforced to groom yourself or your parent grooms you, brushing your teeth, brushing your hair, eating a good breakfast, role playing with friends, having a keen energy to learn and explore the world.
For your efforts generally you're given some sort of reward: affection or love from a family member, sweets, take-away food, processed foods, stickers.
This connects to a concept Skinner called *'operant behaviour'*[7] or *'operant conditioning'*[7]. Where he explained: *'A positive reinforcer strengthens any behavior that produces it'*[7], and: *'A negative reinforcer strengthens any behavior that reduces or terminates it'*[7].
This is where the childhood trauma, or work of the inner child is also relatable as those *'negative reinforcers'*[7] which were generally from a 'trusted' loved one expressing a dislike or dissatisfaction in what you're doing, embedded into your conditioned mind to trigger that particular trauma from childhood later in your evolution.

On the other hand, of these evolutionary processes taking place- at one point you will or have already begun to realise you didn't receive the likely outcome you desired or feel a lack of satisfaction. This generally results in you beginning to display actions of what people call 'puberty', 'teenage moods', 'dark night of the soul', 'the rebel', 'increased risk-taking behaviours', some even label this in the third dimension (as a being) as having a 'behaviour issue' or 'being mentally ill or unstable'. But you begin to test, experiment and question everything you were taught before, everything you were subconsciously conditioned to act as -- you generally begin to do the opposite.

Skinner called this the *'respondent conditioning'* [7] where he wrote: *'contingencies of survival cannot produce useful behaviour if the environment changes substantially from generation to generation, but certain mechanisms have evolved by virtue of which the individual acquires behaviour appropriate to a novel environment during his lifetime'*[7]. He further explained it through an example of, *'the driving force of instincts'*[7] whereby: *'The runner's heart is said to beat fast before the start of the race because he "associates"*[7] *the situation with the exertion which follows'*[7].

So subconsciously you do the opposite of what you were conditioned as a child to do as you begin to inadvertently get a connection inside without consciously realising. Where relating back to Skinner's example of the racing heart effect- From linking your connection of doing consciously the opposite of what you were subconsciously conditioned to do throughout childhood, you associate it with the negative reaction you had from childhood, to the thrill of the racing heart effect. From your *'operant conditioning'*[7] you are now experiencing a scenario to which you are addicted to the pain of the learnt negative reactions from your childhood conditioning.

This notion can be transferable in any interaction you've seen yourself in or can reflect on your 'being's' behaviour now. But you may love the thrill so much that you don't want to consciously recognise this.

Another example is as follows; This can be seen as a negative connection to the *'operant conditioning'*[7] in adult addictions today, such as: gambling, alcohol and substance abuse, materialism and body abuse, disorders of habits, toxic relationships, cheating, lying, stealing, processed food abuse; any egoic negative pattern is due to this sense of a façade thrill of the egoic conditioned mind.

From your conditioned mindset, you either are at a mindset of some sort of state of lack within yourself, and are operating inferiorly, where you do the extreme of the *'operant conditioning'*[7].

 As an example, you work hard in the corporate world, in a job that is not serving your soul but you fear the notion of leaving your job- due to worries of money or gossip of what people would say. Until, you become aware of how your egoic mind has been trained from your childhood into the hierarchical order of the corporate world—you will not awaken to training your own mind out of a *'respondent conditioning'*[7].

The paradigm of this is you may superiorly do the complete opposite of *'operant conditioning'*[7] which is the *'respondent conditioning'*[7] (in this notion): As you become aware of the way in which the corporate world is portrayed in society and begin to find a light in the opposite, where you become fearful of just being another number in the system of the corporate world, and begin to fear being a part of this society- as you awaken to the truth of the hierarchical order. You begin to feel superior, as you awaken to knowing the power of the present moment, the power of spirituality and relating to the notions of religions; becoming a 'zen' figure to yourself. Paradoxically it could be the opposite for you may revert further into a superiority of the *'operant conditioning'*[7], that you know the system and why it is set up the way it is, so you feel as though you are superior to it in this sense, that when you have to go into the third dimensional matrix of the collective to survive, you become fearful and begin to do the opposite in an inferior manner as you feel as though you don't need the matrix. You begin to work on yourself in the fourth dimensional *'respondent conditioning'* [7] where you feel inferior. This notion consists of endeavouring into the corporate world with a sense of belief that; "the knowledge that I have retained, others have not retained", hence making you feel superior. This is a more likely catalyst of your conditioned trained mind, as you endeavour to climb the ranks of the corporate world in your chosen category.

After these cycles, where you awaken into the fourth dimension, you often revert back to the *'operant conditioning'*[7] to heal the inner child: (Any childhood traumas which you have suppressed into your subconscious mind); and you begin to forgive your negative cycles of the *'respondent conditioning'*[7], the in-built egoic patterns of the conditioned mind. You begin to work with the factors in the hope of the 'enlightenment' of life. Without consciously knowing you endeavour into the fifth dimension of the 'conscious', 'healed', 'zen', being to which you were before you were on the Earth.

You can definitely be a pin-ball and revert into the superior *'operant conditioning'*[7] to the inferior *'respondent conditioning'*[7] and vice versa: the inferior *'operant conditioning'*[7] and superior *'respondent conditioning'*[7]; believing to be making progress and feel as if you have repeated it all over again.

But, have no fear, you are right on track!

There's no set number on how many times you have to or will revert, as everyone's evolution is their own and yet paradoxically each of their own is a collective evolution for all.

Healing is necessary and it will happen.

Evolution is necessary and it will happen, and repeating over until you learn and realise each lesson in the situation, is completely necessary also...

Why?

Your evolution, my dearest one.

I haven't even mentioned the best part, a fun game, where the universe will test you to see if you really learnt your lesson or not.

If you have evolved and can identify the lesson prevailing again or if you still need to heal, if so you will learn the lesson of recognising where you need to heal this wound. Generally there's no guide map on how or when you will heal but just know you will and you will retrieve the lesson in the midst of all this.

So what do I mean when I relate your mind conditioning to the ego of the superior or inferior, hence the *'operant conditioning'*[7] and *'respondent conditioning'*[7]?

Well your mind is your past and future analysis of yourself and once you are conditioned by the capitalist stream of the hierarchical system, your ego evolves. Your conditioned mind is on a loop of comparison, competition, judgements, wishful thinking, reflecting, pretty much any sort of unsettling pattern inside of your being, is your conditioned egoic mind.

How is this so?

Your mind is based on the construct of survival. The constant craving to be accepted into a place unknown to you, as this is adapted from your childhood. As you've grown up you have been fed societal 'norms' from parents, friends, teachers, communities on what their projection is on how to behave accordingly in society. They've left imprints (from their grid onto your grid) and these imprints then beat you around for quite a long time. This inner child is needing a healing inside of you, maybe without you even recognising this and appearing in situations through-out your evolution to test you. To make you aware.

But as your subconscious (inner child) mind conflicts with your appearing 'conscious' mind in your life, you begin to unlock the secrets to your necessary healing and become more aware or you may feed it with an inferior *'operant conditioning'*[7] where you find yourself engaging with addictive behaviours in attempt to 'soothe' your 'pain', pushing you further into your subconscious level of the inner child. This same 'soothing' of your 'pain' pushes you even further into creating another layer of the appearing 'conscious' adult, where you end up completely unconsciously living your life. You begin to revert back and forth from inferior *'operant conditioning'*[7] of the 'hierarchy system'—thinking to yourself 'how will I escape? But I have debts, a mortgage, children, concluding to yourself you have no choice—and hence succumbing to the inferior *'respondent conditioning'*[7] of the mind, to which you think- "when I am in control of my assets, I am different to others in society". Yet, you are following the chain of this paradox where everyone follows the exact same lifestyle. You begin to feel in control and hence different, but it is the exact same rat race and life cycle of the ones you thought you were different to.

That's the matriarchal paradigm your conditioned mind is caught in.

Carl G Jung wrote: 'If a man is a neurotic, he has lost confidence in himself. A neurosis is a humiliating defeat and is felt as such by people who are not entirely unconscious of their own psychology. And one is defeated by something "unreal"'[8].

The spirituality revelation today and throughout history with various religions, comprises of the notion of how we have our soul (which is our fifth dimensional spirit), our mind (our fourth dimensional ego) and our body (third dimensional physical). The ego being our conditioned (reptilian brain) where we have subconscious (either natural or nurtured) incoming thoughts where we compare, analyse and suggest the ways in which we act. If we are not carefully conscious of this process, we can end up sleepwalking only thinking about our demands and being completely unconsciously addicted to this narcissistic way of living, where we are our number one priorities for our third dimensional demands. Our third-dimensional demands meaning the conditioning in-built into us based upon a thought of lack.

 To which could be observed in your own evolution, as you realise the regard to which you function day-to-day. Or maybe you will notice it now you have read it here.

In general, within your mind you will then have a battle with yourself. The questions will arise about yourself being in your mindset of conditioned capitalist. You may question, but if I do this in the third dimension now it will advance me into a fourth dimension of progression and then to the fifth. But there's a flaw; is your mind being brought back to a third dimensional grounded state still searching for the next thing or object or materialism to attempt to advance you into the fourth dimension asking the exact same questions, looking for another alternative? This is your addictive state, your conditioned egoistic, narcissistic state where your mind is governing you subconsciously, without your 'being', being consciously aware of it. You're stuck questioning if you're really making progress, completely unaware whether you are fulfilled or not, completely out of touch with your soul. But fear not as this is completely natural for your evolutionary purpose.

---

[8] Jung (1958), p.10.

Elias Lake Tolbert wrote: 'Conseling helps the pupil decide what other aspects of education mean for him and what he should do about them'[9].

In this life, this evolutionary process, you can see yourself as your own counsellor. You are the one who will turn around at the end of your days and say that everything was necessary, that you had no regrets and that you're glad you never gave up (hopefully). When you realise your ego, your conditioned mind, your patterns, your behaviours innately learned, your subconscious mindset, what makes you tick; Just reflect, you discover your power, your truth, your fulfilment, what's worthy of your time, what's not worthy of your time, what your drive is, what motivates you, what chills you out in those unconscious emotional highs. All of it is your power.

There's no greater beauty than realising your soul purpose and sharing it positively with the world. A 'bad' guy can still be a 'good' guy in their own evolution if they acknowledge this 'badness' and relate it to the world, alchemising their purpose into being completely vulnerable to connect with their (soul) heart space to help those beneath them. Not to display anyone as a 'bad' or 'good' guy- but those who go through addictive behaviours, learn from their experience and share it with the world in a beneficial way through being vulnerable, completely alchemising and recreating themselves to realign with their soul purpose and evolution.

This is just an example although it is said in ancient African cultures about the 'dark night of the soul', the breaking away of conforming to the tribe. The evolutionary process of breaking from your childhood mindset and conditioned societal beliefs to realign with your soul purpose. This can also be seen in the expression of art and artists, through the way in which they evolve in the third dimensional matriarchal society construct.

As a brief example, women and men are told how their body should look, how love should be, how this improves their skin or face, this will improve your dating, this will improve the way you dress, walk, talk: to essentially play on your insecurities of not wanting to fit into the *'operant conditioning'*[7] of your

---

[9] Tolbert (1959), p.vii.

childhood. This is where the capitalist corporations make their money, as they thrive on the catastrophe, thriving on 'the dark night of the soul', the appearing awakening, all in an attempt to superficially numb some yearning inside of you caused by your inner child reaching out for help and hence caused by the initial hierarchical system that was enforced consciously on you as a child.

But have no fear.
Don't freak out just yet.
Pin-balling back and forth, evolutionising, realising none of these egoic mind patterns are serving you and then going within to discover the true unresolved issues within your soul. This will then lead you into alignment with your soul's purpose again. With the universes' intentions for you. There's a yin and yang, a good and bad to everything. Sure your mind will now be reading this thinking- "How do I escape going into these patterns?" "How do I get out of the matrix?" "How do I find my purpose right now?".
Relax.
Chill.
Deep breath.
You've got this, it's been inside you this whole time.
You can't escape it, unless you feel like being a recluse in a cave for the rest of your life.
No, it is all necessary.
But once you realise that, you won't be scared of failing or 'messing' up, because there is no 'mess-ups' anymore.
You'll realise what that little voice yearns for once you've paid it attention and healed it, and within that you then will find just how you will contribute to the world.
Maybe you'll be a hero, maybe you'll be a villain, but although if you've left this body learning your lesson and contributing to the unconditional stream of love in the universe, you've definitely succeeded in your evolutionary purpose.

I'm not saying life is easy, because we all know some days you'll feel like banging your head against a brick wall, but it's necessary. It's happening everyday, yet everyday paradoxically nothing is happening at all. You think your issues are issues, that it is the end of the world as you know it, because you're conditioned from a child to be 'spoon-fed' solutions. It is time to embrace your power with the whole 'being' you are now.

In conclusion, this chapter -- the catastrophe of the conditioned mind, well indeed we know it can be a catastrophe, a complete traumatic, memorable experience from the time you were put on Earth in this physical body, because your conditioned mind is programmed from your childhood to think on a basis from Gregg Braden's conclusions of: *'competition, conflict, struggle and scarcity'*[4] due to society's capitalist, hierarchical demands. The whole democratic system is based upon hierarchies, the world is based upon a notion of extremes, because with extremes you can distinguish and create a separation of: wealthy to non-wealthy countries, first-world countries to third-world countries, healthy foods to non-healthy foods: all complete extremes of the ego, hence your conditioned mind. You're taught from a young age to process this type of information, if you don't you won't do well in school, hence you won't get a good job, hence you won't make lots of money, hence you won't survive in the economy.

It's all based upon Herman Hollerith's tabulating and sorting machines to determine how much you thrive, on how you are going to be sorted into the current capitalist system. At school you have a report paper to say how well you did in each subject, how much information you could retain, you then move into secondary school where they give you 'freedom' to choose some subjects, to in turn then see again how much information you can retain and then sort you into these categories for your university degrees, to then further test your university degrees, then then further test you again on how much information you can retain. Each time believing and striving for better scores, whilst you make the different education systems look good or bad, to hold up the systems' eliteness. Further, once finished a degree, you get out of university and apply for a working position, to further contribute to the system of capitalism (that is already in place) and sell your lifespan to a company, believing you are growing 'richer' in society's eyes. You trade your physical body and capabilities in return for a decimal point on a slip of paper to pay off the things you are in a decimal point negative to and buy the things that the capitalists' system has put a price on to keep you in the same system that upholds the hierarchy.

This is the catastrophe of the mind, the negative.

The next chapter, The Subtle War on Information, talks of how this catastrophe is affecting your relationship with your being, other beings and your universe.

III.   The Subtle War on Information.

'Sociologists have found that our home addresses, our friends, our clubs, our values, and even our church affiliations can prove to be "barriers" if we fail to change them with every attempted move up the ladder. This is a most disheartening situation to find in the nation that poses as the model for the democratic world'[10].

Abraham Maslow constructed basic needs for a being to self-actualise in 1968. He wrote: *'The basic needs (for life, for safety and security, for belongingness and affection, for respect and self-respect, and for self-actualization)'"[11].* Maslow is an important aspect when becoming aware of how your conditioned mind is reactive in situations, as you can begin to grasp where your conditioned mind is lacking an aspect, and how to alchemise this to attain self worth. This is especially essential when analysing the component of the need for love and belonging, as once you are aware of this biological need, you can then attain the requirements of your needs through yourself, from source.

The notion of war is generally the aftermath of a disagreement between two parties. It could be countries, animals, humans, yourself and in pretty much any context of homes, schools, workplaces, in a coffee shop, in traffic, in a zoo, in the wild, desert, anywhere. And you, wherever you are, whatever you're doing are in a war of information, as this is the new-age war.

When you are born, you are placed into a category, information is taken, based upon your physical external appearances and the portal you came from; i.e. your mother and carers. The geographics, the surroundings of where you came from and how it fits in the system's hierarchical map. You are then enforced with what health care systems expect and in an inferior state your carer will reluctantly succumb to the war of information, providing you with the nutrients and health care 'pre-cautions' they have been conditioned to believe, or vice versa to superiorly go against the third dimensional information of capitalism and provide you with their research of what you need as a child.
Once you attend school it's an extreme of the *'operant conditioning'[7]* you have

---

[10] Packard, V. (1961), p.4.
[11] Maslow, A.H. (1968), p.3.

just received and in some cases individuals have reverted to the *'respondent conditioning'*[7] first, which drives their carers to believe they have some sort of abnormality as they are 'different' to the 'status quo' of conditioning—often children (even adults) can be labelled as attention deficit and hyperactivity disorders (ADHD), autistic, suffering from learning disabilities, learning difficulties, even mentally ill as young as they're born, often to test carers, parents and societies on themselves and show them their reflections of their own extreme conditioned state. It's a 'no-brainer' that individuals are ostracised from the community of the world once they challenge everything you once believed true. As there is no true or false, everything is ever-changing, ever-evolving, ever-repeating until we've learnt the lesson, and even then life tests you repeatedly. From school you are conditioned operantly, in high school generally naturally evolution of the body kicks in to challenge this view and you generally resist *'operant conditioning'*[7] through *'respondent conditioning'*[7]. Birth and death physically from others close to you or mentally yourself generally brings a certain pain which tests your 'respondent conditioning'[7] and 'operant conditioning'[7] process.

Through these tests and questioning, which some people call 'spiritual awakening', 'coming back to God', 'leaving the tribe', it generally brings about a sense of coming back into alignment with your higher purpose, your soul evolutionary process and in these times you begin to find lessons. But before this, especially with the internet having a search engine to check facts and social forums that allow you to stalk, peep, gossip and 'connect' with what other individuals are doing, here we have a society based upon this notion of the egoic construction once again.

It's a subconscious conditioning which you don't even know is happening to you, but it's happening all around you and in you, causing you to have a subconscious yearning and suffering outlook. When looking on certain apps at the recent updates of your virtual connections (for example), you are comparing yourself to other people's lives, judging others on your different journeys. Judging someone else as if everyone is on the exact same journey as you. Slowly programming your mind to thinking you could do this better, be a bit more like this, less like this; you do it without even realising. I wonder how many times an individual checks their phone a day? It's addicting this inner child need, to feel needed, this false love, it is designed to be addicting. Not only this notion of yearning begins to tear relationships apart, the heart centre apart, through the notion of jealousy. When looking on social media platforms today, it shows you who has been online, who has been liking things, who has been commenting, what they're liking, commenting, following, who people have been with and what their doing. If you have a neglected inner child in need of healing and don't feel secure in yourself, you will succumb to the war on information. An example would entail; Throwing questions at your partner such as; "Why have you been online- I thought you were asleep?" "Why are you liking this person's photos?" "Why are you at this place? I thought you were here..." "Why did you tag this person in a meme?" Or seeing your friends online, possibly asking similar questions or family members. An infinite loop of non-rewarding patterns where you intend to remark without saying it, "I don't trust you". If you cannot trust their relationship with you, whether it be a friend, colleague or partner, how do you love someone? How do you love yourself?

Where there appears to be no love, there is love with conditions, which turns into a war of fighting for someone's love and trust. It's an unresolved issue within you, a test for you, yet we get so stuck in externalising the issue onto the other person. That we believe their actions are what has caused this, as we are not aware of the overall evolutionary process. Their actions or relationship with you in that particular time and space displays the lesson needed for you to evolve, once you learn this lesson and heal the pain inside you, you can proceed in your evolutionary mission, your purpose, what you came to earth to truly be. In no way is that a call to hold onto someone who is mentally or emotionally or physically abusing your unconditional love, sometimes the best lesson learnt is the one where you realise they've served their purpose, showed you what you needed to evolve in and now it's time to move on without them, in the third dimension.

'So if we have been able to transform our minds we will have actually received the spiritual master's blessings in the true sense of the word'. –Dalai Lama[12].

Once you've identified the bad patterns your conditioned mind (reptilian brain) plays on you and your actions convey, you will feel the emotions boiling as you try to push this feeling away. You realise the true potential of your heart. You'll

---

[12] Lama, D. (1995),pxv-65.

cry and scream and realise your heart connection again, and that this third dimensional conditioning, these negative egoic urges and narcissistic traits, aren't serving you anymore. You become more trusting in others, you can look into their eyes and truly listen to what they're saying. Sure you can make a healthy judgement from your own morals but you truly see the other person's heart space and what character role they came to play in your life. Sometimes it's the best healing there is, to say that person loved me so much they came down to play the villain in my evolution so I could proceed, is sometimes all the healing, love and detachment you desire for another being in this universe.

'A selfish attitude creates fear and insecurity which in turn creates distrust. So even for the people who have no special faith, it is important to have a peaceful mind'. – Dalai Lama[12].

Holding a space for hate in your heart only creates a distrust between yourself. You being to wonder "why me?" "Why do these things happen to me?", the anger, the fear of feeling it may happen again, "what's the point?". You eventually begin to not trust the world or other people, a rising fear blossoms in front of you, looking like a protection barrier but inside having the stench of hay-fever in the spring time. You eventually get yourself sick, ill at the mere grasp of the fear your conditioned mind plays. This hate, this angst, only creates a separation between yourself as you begin to be further and further disconnected from your evolutionary process, repeating over the same unhealthy mindset of "why these situations keep happening", literally attracting the same vibrational frequencies until you learn the lesson to enhance your vibrational frequency. This insecurity and fearful state of your conditioned mind becomes a magnet for similar situations and events until you've grasped the lesson, in order to advance your being spiritually, mentally and physically. If you have succumb to this trap of the conditioning where you are in a negative mindset, in order to advance yourself, the only way is within.

If the war on information from the outside and other beings wasn't difficult enough, well you now may endeavour into your internal war on information. Many debates of the nature versus nurture and where you get your information from can be seen throughout history, but once you take your own power back, you realise the only limitation is you.
For some that is scary, but it's also empowering.

Once you realise your thought patterns, and are aware of when your egoic nature of the conditioned mind comes into play, you can then realise and back track your negative mental patterns of the inferior and superior behaviour. Those same mental habits that are detrimental to your evolutionary purpose, where you act on your irrational, egoic, impulsive, addicting, narcissistic ideas, that big voice in your head that sometimes dominates your actions. These you can give recognition to and distinguish them from your true authenticity.
You can distinguish the voices from outsider's projections, to your intuition- your gut feeling.
Most likely in your mind you'll have an inferior (operant conditioned) voice, a

superior (respondent conditioned) voice in your conditioned mind, which are helpful in getting you into situations early on, so you can evolve into your ever-growing evolutionary purpose and learn the lessons you need to attain in this third dimensional 'reality'. Although the fifth dimension is the slight feelings in your abdomen in your sensational body, your intuitive nature, where you just know you're on a path that will benefit you for your highest good.

The next chapter, The Channelings of the Soul, alchemises the chapter about the catastrophe of the mind in relation to the *'operant conditioning'*[7] and *'respondent conditioning'*[7], into a more positive light.

IV.   The Channelings of the Soul.

The alchemy of the catastrophe of the conditioned mind is where the positive light to this inner child comes through telling you it needs help.
The solution, is you.
I could finish the chapter there but I know the mind demands elaboration.

In Rhodes' book *'The Evolution of Life'* he opens; *'Chapter 9 The Dominance of the Reptiles' with: 'We have already seen in some of the ways in which the reptile body differs from that of the amphibian, and in terms of mode of life and range of possible habitats the difference is equally profound. The amphibian were limited to swamps and lowland marshes; in these environments the reptiles replaced and excelled them in their adaptation. But the advent of the reptiles also marked the vertebrates' invasion of other environments, some totally new- forests, and deserts, the seas and the air. It is this widespread adaptation and diversity over a period of one hundred and fifty million years that is the measure of the reptiles' success. In the long history of life only two other groups, the mammals and the birds, have achieved anything approaching such a diversity of adaptation; and even their success is an indirect tribute to their reptilian ancestors'*[13].

Your mind will either say conspiracy theory or freak out thinking what if I'm a reptile.
Chill for a second.
You've come this far, maybe in your last life you played the role of a dolphin, a shark, a priest, a murderer, whatever it was, your past has got you to this specific point in your evolution right now. The same as your conditioning in the third dimensional construct of the collective. The experiences you have faced, you may have been bullied as a child, had cancer as an adult, your dad may have passed away, whatever the event the universe has decided to give you for your evolution in the past, has got you to this exact moment in space and time to evolutionise further. Even if you are reading this book, there is an inner yearning to evolve further.

Gandhi[14] *said: 'To forgive is not to forget. The merit lies in loving in spite of the vivid knowledge that the one that must be loved is not a friend. There is no merit in loving an*

---

[13] Rhodes, F.H.T. (1962), p.185.
[14] Bhalla, S. (1920), p.17.

enemy when you forget him for a friend'.

The mind tends to overanalyse, label the characters in the events (people) as the issues, attaching them to a particular triggered emotion within you, in accordance to thrive from the inside. This is how your egoic conditioned reptilian mind thrives. That externally there are threats. Yes, it can be good in order to survive in the human body as you will probably analyse a threat if you were to throw yourself into a lion's territory, but for the purpose of connecting back to yourself, having this mindset is not particularly helpful. In order to channel your soul in situations where you scream wondering what your purpose is, you need to connect. To connect to the universe is to connect to yourself. Wondering why or shouting or blaming other people will only hide you from yourself further, as you identify further and further with an emotional trigger. This emotional trigger isn't you. Sure it may be inside of you, and sure you may have a belief of "well why is it only triggered by this one person?". This is your *'operant conditioning'⁷*, the catastrophe of the conditioned mind coming into effect, realising the conditioning of cause and effect, if I do this in turn this will happen.
The A to B plan.
Not connecting with the higher plan for yourself, which is hard, because I've never met a person who can 100% tell you their lifespan at the age of two, exactly what would happen, because then you would already know the lessons you need to learn. But think about it, your success rate on getting your soul this far in your evolutionary process is 100% to this day... So there has to be something higher, this is the quantum realm, the law of attraction, the wisdom (information) era, you know this to be true when you look in your heart.
Blaming people for your evolutionary purpose will only eventuate into an event where there's no way to blame someone for your evolution, but hey sometimes this is necessary. Ex-addicts (of any type of abuse) will probably tell you the best way to rise is to hit rock bottom, it's necessary. Then, in that rock bottom moment, when you cry and scream, feel sorry for yourself, wonder how and why you got to this stage, you realise that this is the only way up, you suddenly fall back on something greater than the victim story you have been telling yourself in the past, something even greater than yourself, it's what the Western Society labels as God, the Universe, the God-like force, or what churches label as different pseudonyms for the Universal Force. In this mind conditioned labelling of 'knowing' or thinking "this is the worst situation that I've got myself into"- once you change your mindset and alchemise the situation, it can also be the best

situation you have encountered, as you can now be grateful for the lesson it has taught you and how to proceed.

That last straw of the conditioned mind where you know the external does not work anymore. Sure it could be addictions to money, drugs, alcohol abuse, materialistic objects, beauty objects, sex, travelling; you realise suddenly that all these gateways to the matrix, to succumbing to the materialistic third dimensional world, it just isn't getting you to where you would like to be, anymore. You often don't know where that place even is, where you would like to be, but you realise this just isn't the answer anymore. I think maybe that's what the spiritual ego forced upon society and children tend to forget, that there has to be a downfall, a conditioning to the society which is in place today, for one to realise that's not the answer they seek. That the '9-5 grind' is not what we came here to do. Or maybe it is what you came here to do in order for others to see their reflections amplified and realise that's not what they came here to do— then lesson learnt.

But if you're reading this book I gather you're a bit 'lost' as the mind labels it or needing a sign subconsciously to further justify your already attained knowledge from within; A little more guidance you may seek from this.

In the previous chapter I have broken down the catastrophe of the conditioned mind, and yes where you're hidden behind your conditioned mind and realise it, it can be daunting, an infinite loop in your head of a spiritual ego that attains knowledge on why you think the way you do, and whose to blame, maybe your conditioned mind will blame the government or your family, or societal structures, cultural beliefs, going round and round justifying your current state of mind, with your previous events. But to come back to your soul, your heart space, you realise all that got you to where you are now, pride, your ego on how gracefully you let go of the events you encountered and how beautifully you learnt your lessons and proceed. There's not much else to say really. Those people, society, organisations, your conditioned mind blames, is the same mind that put you in those situations, manifesting those character roles, to learn the lessons you know now. Sure you may take a *'respondent conditioning'*[7] whereby you are inferior or superior to the event, through your emotions. But once you realise you are not the emotions you are feeling, you are the lesson that manifests, you become merely an observer of the events which your subconscious mind has manifested for you. Like watching a movie, where you're in it. You begin to detach from the people and places and the materialistic objects of the third dimension, to rely on faith of the fifth to advance yourself in the fourth. Your lessons become the tool to connect with your soul and evolutionary purpose, in order to become stronger in your evolutionary mission, for the next tests, and stronger to observe your conditioning in the third dimensional matriarchal system. Detaching from your emotional triggers and letting the energy run through you, allows you to realise the energetic role that person plays in your life, why you manifested them and how to proceed. The only way to proceed is being apprehensive about your soul mission, becoming aware, awakening to what your goal is on earth, how you'll work it for you.

The only way is to begin to channel your soul, not through an ego or spiritual ego but through those still moments, when you know you're on the right path. What's good for your 'being'. Those moments where you don't have to question yourself, you just know. That's where you've channelled your true authenticity, your evolutionary process, your reason for being. It's not to know everything or find all the answers, but to trust that it is eventuating to the place that you return home.
Returning to yourself.
To save yourself from your conditioned self is to let it be, finding peace in life's chaos.
Cést la vie.

V.   The Movement to Love.

'There can be no unity without love. Love is the key that opens all doors. Love is the balm that heals all wounds. Love is the light that lightens the darkness. Love draws together, makes whole, creates oneness. Love makes us want to give and give- of our talents, our service, our lives. Love makes life worth living. Where there is love there is peace. When we love one another we will no longer stand back and criticise other people's way of life, their religion, rituals, beliefs, traditions. When we are at peace within ourselves, we will no longer try to change others, and we will no longer be frightened of our differences'[15] - *Eileen Caddy.*

The psychology behind this chapter relates to Maslow's hierarchy of needs whereby Maslow believed in order to reach *'self-actualisation'*[11] a human had to have four basic needs accounted for: physiological, safety, love and belonging, and esteem. Some spiritualists believe we have been 5000 years in love then 5000 years in power, then 5000 years in the wisdom age, that the Mayan's predicted as 'the age of Aquarius', the start of a new world order. Whatever it is you have found a truth in, we are all achieving the same goal: a revolution in love.

We have realised there are extremes in wisdom from extremes in power, and as a result the only way forward, to move into harmony is to repeat history, the history of moving to love. The connection with the universe, God, history, yourself, nature, animals; These are all aligning to create a connection in love. The notion of understanding one another, the way the world works and coming back to yourself enables you to become not just a product of the matriarchal system, but create a new world order for yourself.
Learning to love again, without the egoic notion of loving with conditions, or penalising someone in your mind as them being a narcissist or other egoic blockages to further entice the role they played in your evolutionary purpose. The more you disconnect with the meaning, the more you manifest the exact same situation but with a different scenery, circumstances and characters. The universe, your subconscious mind will manifest and test you on the lessons you need to learn in order to grow in your evolution, this is the way it works, this is life.

You unlock this subconscious pattern, into your conscious being, you then allow

---

[15] Caddy, E. (1988), p.8.

yourself to realise the answers you were seeking this whole time. You will realise why it happened the way it did and you can then come back to the loving vibration of understanding the situation, the roles, the characters played and what lessons of yourself is to be learnt.

You'll forgive.

You'll forgive yourself for victimising your being and others.

You'll forgive the humans who played the characters in your life, for you'll understand why you subconsciously manifested the event.

You'll learn the lesson that your subconscious mind wanted to portray to you, maybe it's a trauma to address from your childhood, maybe it's to wake you up from your conditioned mind, maybe it's to make you realise your own power; however, you will see a lesson within.

After this you will learn to be grateful for the experience, for if it never happened you would not be as advanced in your evolutionary purpose, as you are today. In this grateful nature you'll find peace, you'll find a snippet of a peace of mind that makes you realise this calmness of the necessity. A sense of trust follows, a little empowerment feeling, where you realise the reason for it all and now that you've acknowledged it you can see the bigger picture, that everything happens for a reason and you rely on a sense of a higher power.

Then comes the love, you begin to love what happened at first maybe the characters, as your mind identifies that they were the reason for your evolution, until you're thrown within another event to test you and allow you to realise your own power.

Then you may begin to love the cycle, the feeling of the pleasure and pain cycle and you may even repeat this over to the extremity with different circumstances, until this also inevitably doesn't work. But fear not, as you can have trust in the evolutionary process of your being. Then a certain sense of a true love. A non-addicting, non-egoic, non-conditioned, sort of love that allows you to still grow in yourself but find independence in your own evolution and hence spread a sort of service to others on their evolutionary process also. This is your soul purpose, aligning yourself with unconditional love, for the third, fourth and fifth dimension, for your being, the past, present and future you, for forgiving yourself and the world and people, every single day, minute, second: Having a 'New Year resolution' every minute, to love the world and the universe- which is you.

The animals are you.

The nature is you.

The world is you.

The universe is you.

Every single situation in your life, you have subconsciously created to wake you to your soul purpose. Each lesson allows you to be back in alignment with your soul mission, your own universal map, already written for you, followed for you. You are it and it is you.
You are the one you have been yearning for.
It's all in your heart.
The answers you seek are within.

'My bounty is as boundless as the sea, My love as deep. The more I give to thee, The more I have, for both are infinite'[16].

The more you 'lose' yourself- by 'losing' yourself I mean your three dimensional, conditioned, materialistic, matriarchal slave type self, everything 'you knew' for sure, to be your truth- The more you dig, the more you learn. The more you grow. The more you begin to come back to the fourth dimensional way of grinding for your meaning. The discovery of coming back to your purpose. You realise what you have to offer the world, how to benefit the third dimension matriarchy system, by bringing in the fifth dimension from within and transmuting it into the evolutionary outlook of the fourth dimension. This is where you work on yourself each day to benefit the third dimension. When you have endeavoured deep into the work of serving others, or even yourself, this is where you will begin to channel your soul purpose. For you will realise the materialism of the third dimension only makes you happy for a certain time period, is happiness your goal? To know happiness you'll compare it to your sadness, wouldn't you rather be at peace? Maybe this could be your goal. This is where your growth develops. You question yourself developing this spiritual, knowledge driven ego, until you escape it all by utilising your ego as a tool for your soul purpose. Priding yourself on the love your heart has created, attracted and evolved in.
You have the power, the power to break free of your conditioned mind, the power to trust, to listen, to love again. The power is within you already. The answers lie within the beholder, you.

---

[16] Kerrigan, M. (2003). *Shakespeare on Love.* Penguin Books Australia.

'All I really need to know about how to live and what to do and how to be I learned in kindergarten. Wisdom was not at the top of the graduate-school mountain, but there in the sandpile at the Sunday School. These are the things I learned:

Share everything.

Play fair.

Don't hit people.

Put things back where you found them.

Clean up your own mess.

Don't take things that aren't yours.

Say you're sorry when you hurt somebody.

Wash your hands before you eat.

Flush.

Warm cookies and cold milk are good for you.

Live a balanced life- learn some and think some and draw and paint and sing and dance and play and work every day some.

Take a nap every afternoon.

When you go out into the world, watch out for traffic, hold hands and stick together.

Be aware of wonder.

Remember the little seed in the Styrofoam cup: The roots go down and the plant goes up and nobody really knows how or why, but we are all like that. Goldfish and hamsters and white mice and even the little seed in the Styrofoam cup- they all die.

So do we.

And then remember the Dick-and-Jane books and the first word you learned- the biggest word of all- LOOK.

Everything you need to know is in there somewhere. The Golden Rule and love and basic sanitation. Ecology and politics and equality and sane living.

Take any one of those items and extrapolate it into sophisticated adult terms and apply it to your family life or your work or your government or your world and it holds true and clear and firm. Think what a better world it would be if we all – the whole world – had cookies and milk about three o'clock every afternoon and then lay down with our blankies for a nap. Or if all governments had as a basic policy to always put things back where they found them and to clean up their own mess.

And it is still true, no matter how old you are – when you go out into the world, it is best to hold hands and stick together'. - Fulgham[17].

Through the basis of analysing what you learnt in kindergarten, you can adapt how it depicts every lesson you need to know as an adult. There is a whole universe inside you that has manifested these lessons early on and until you've learnt the lessons they keep on manifesting themselves in your three dimensional life until you become grateful for them. What the Greeks have noted as the circle of life- it will continue over and over until you've mastered it. The only way

---

[17] Fulgham, R. (1989). *All I Really Need to Know I Learned in Kindergarten: Uncommon Thoughts on Common Things.* Grafton Books.

forwards – is to go backwards, and to give recognition as to why certain events are structured the way they are is essential in order to move beyond, hence alchemising your evolutionary purpose.

This is where your true power lies.

Realising the essence of moving into a loving vibration of yours and others evolutionary purpose, what role they play in theirs, to grasping your own vibration and authenticity. Forgiving yourself over and over, and forgiving others over and over to detach from an egoic victim story and alchemise it into your evolution in a positive manner. The yin and yang.

Loving it all with no regrets or giving a label to anything as a mistake or carrying an energetic body from the past into your present. To release it all and embrace the higher realm of unconditional love. That's where your true power lies. Not within seeking lessons, but releasing them from your being. Releasing all the labels society portrays that you should feel, the ones that relate to Gregg Braden's conclusion of *'competition, conflict, struggle and scarcity'* [4]. The conditioned, societal, matriarchal, third dimensional model of 'being', the presence of the materialistic realm of being present. A system that thrives on you not understanding. It's forgiving this system you were groomed into and alchemising it to benefit those past and future souls, and your present soul.

This is the way to love.

VI.   The Tool of Vulnerability.

Having a sensitive heart in a world of chaos is the answer to the truth you seek. For in having a sensitive heart, you become less egoic in your catastrophes of your mind. You begin to realise that succumbing to the superiority of your conditioning will only hurt yourself and betray your own being. As everyone is a reflection of you, in some way.

On the contrary, you may be belittling yourself to an inferior position, but when your mindset sees you in an inferior position and less egoic, you realise when you alternate into your superiority, hence you can uncover the fluctuations between your egoic conditioned mind. Which brings you closer to a state of a growth mindset, where you can identify your egoic patterns within your being. Further dis-identifying with your victim story as you can revert back to your empathetic nature. The empathetic nature of your being is then felt towards those involved in your circumstances, events, characters, and hence becomes an energetic-body of this empathetic nature that you begin to carry into your future events and situations. Raising your vibration from the lessons, to attract a higher lesson and vibrational force.

To utilise your vulnerability in any situation in your life allows you to express the energy running through you. This energy often demands your attention, as you eventually develop in your natural state of being. Otherwise holding onto these energies advances into you letting it out in a different situation and hence manifesting subconsciously a recurring situation, without you possibly being aware of this. An infinite loop of the same circle, the recurring 'dark night of the soul', the catastrophe of your conditioned mind, running in the direction of a fearful nature.

The next stage could potentially be a fearful 'respondent conditioning'[7] of inferiority or superiority, where you define your heart as being inferior due to being open, where you are aware of the fearful nature of someone hurting you, as you 'wear your heart on your sleeve'. You begin to relate it to something that happened a while ago, or fearful of something that may happen, both being completely illusory. The egoic conditioned mind playing out the victim story in your head, about a past childhood trauma, that you'd never completely let go of the energy yet. You've trapped this energy from the quantum (astral) realm inside your genetic DNA make-up, identifying with it as you. Never letting that energy pass through you, nor making peace with it, for a subconscious fear that you won't know who you are, you won't know your identity. Eckhart Tolle speaks of this as the 'pain-body'[1]; each time you subconsciously manifest a lesson to bring up that 'pain-body'[1] awareness you feed that 'pain-body'[1] more fuel identifying an outside energy with who you are.

Yes, it's hard to let go of such traumatic events, but is it really necessary to hold onto it, identify it with your soul? Your own spiritual being? The external event manifested into your evolutionary process to teach you a lesson, bringing about external energies, you hold onto instead of merely allowing them to pass through you?

The acting industry is taught the emotional tone scale, where there are adaptations, but mainly it explores how emotions are energy in motion. If you observe artists, actors, comedians, performers, you'll find they can manifest from their subconscious into their conscious; an energy that allows a whole audience to feel what they feel. They can alter the energy in motion. Although this is also how they become confused in what is truly coming from them and what's just for the stage, but everyone is a piece of artwork. Everyone is picking up on body language, emotions (energy) and cues, from others, all day, everyday. You could be standing on the train and someone could be trying to read you, what your motives are, 'sussing you out', people just do this either in an overly superior or under inferior trusting way, that they often feel it's easier to detach from other beings and situations, becoming consumed within their own conditioned mind.

If you alchemise the mainstream media, it actually brings about an energy that makes you feel empathic towards others' situations, for a short while, before you go back to your '9-5 grind' matriarchal state of the third dimensional construct. Although majority of the mainstream media is negative, it does enable you to observe the emotional tone scale, if you escape your own fear-based reptilian mind-set. If you are aware and strong in your own power, you can awaken to alchemising the fear-based three dimensional reality.
You change yourself and you can change the world.
Everyone has a conditioned mind, operantly conditioned through fear, either from parents, teachers, family, society, as written about in the previous chapters; However, once you are aware of your own traits and recognise them, no matter how 'bad' or 'good' society labels them as, you will uncover the secret to your evolutionary purpose.

A vulnerable heart can be your greatest tool, as it is the complete opposite to a detached, closed off heart. A vulnerable heart allows you to feel love and that is the source of your 'self-actualisation'[11], your soul purpose, that's where you will help the world and yourself evolve.

Imagine if every being spoke their truth and empathised with a loving vibration towards other people's opinions- I'm sure we would reach a lot more solutions rather than jumping to egoic conclusions and creating temporary solutions.
As stated in the previous chapter about 'The War on Information', having a vulnerable vibration in your heart-space will attract an unconditional love into

the space and love wins all. It will prevail and conquer in those times you think "what's the point?", your heart will wear a metaphorical vulnerability sticker and you will find your power—you will say what you mean and mean what you say.

Nothing is more powerful than looking at yourself in the mirror, looking deep into your own soul, knowing you've spoken your truth that day and you've spread unconditional love, in those times your ego was screaming inside. Despite it all the unconditional love of your vulnerable heart, is not attached to a situation or a thing. Your heart set the way, it led by example, you paved the way of the desired demand of your vibration. The universe may place in your way situations to test your evolutionary progress, or test you with higher or lower vibrations to allow you to grow or learn your lesson of being in your own power. These are all lessons to consider when evaluating your evolutionary process or even if you are in fear of having a vulnerable heart shown to the world, it can be your greatest strength if you allow it to be. Through great courage comes your strength.

If you allow yourself to be aware of your conditioned mind patterns through recognising your triggers, those moments where you know something is your weakness and you can detach an emotional charge to something else, you will conquer your evolution. When you deter from reacting on an attached energetic force from the past or future into the current moment, this will further allow you to effectively conclude the situation; as you've recognised the subconscious limiting belief (the pattern) and further allowed yourself to prevail to acknowledge the energy and communicate it through alchemy to the situation. This is a beneficial goal to have in your evolution, this type of awareness and tool of alchemy. Communicating the energy in motion to those involved in the situation can also be beneficial to the event, as you acknowledge how this event makes your 'being' react and how you can further move past this, to learn the lesson your 'being' needs. It also saves your conditioned mind and those involved, in your manifested events, from their conditioned mind within their beings, as they realise why this energy is manifested inside themselves when they are in this situation around you. They'll know what to learn and how to move forward (with or without you) and into a more loving vibration, where they're on their soul paths also.

There is a trap that a vulnerable heart can also fall into, where thinking if you speak your mind you'll hurt those involved. This trap is a superiority approach, where you feel as though you have an increased awareness of emotional recognition and attempt to save the other in the event. Although you'll soon realise that through trying to save everyone you aren't doing yourself or them any justice, as you are steering them off their soul path and you off your own, as you aren't in your true authentic nature. This is the downfall of the empath, the hero, the healer, if you believe you can 'save' everyone, you succumb to a selfish mindset, as it's impossible to 'save' everyone, as no one can save anyone, they can only save themselves and lead by example. This is also where the superiority of the egoic conditioned mind of the *'operant conditioning'*[7] can also come into effect, as you begin to be fearful of evolving yourself, so you succumb to the three-dimensional matriarchal system of staying in the cycle of the expected, thinking this will save you, something to live for, you're more advanced this way, having a plan of the future contexts. You're also in a trap this way, as you're governed by fear. The day you allow yourself to let go of the energies inside you and around you that aren't serving your evolutionary purpose anymore, is the day you begin to heal.

You begin to give recognition to those mindsets that society subconsciously deems as unrecognisable, not worthy, not necessary, out of character. This is where you create an infancy of flow of a new mindset, a trust in the process of your unfolding worthiness of your soul. The beauty of love will flow from this and you'll soon align with the stillness and hence the connectedness to everything.

Being vulnerable in a situation, allows you to connect with other beings on their journeys. Whether it be nature, animals or other humans, you will feel a sense of home, of connection, of empathetic vibrations; where you feel you're understood, loved, accepted- mainly animals and nature are prime examples of allowing you to sympathetically vibrate at one, in eachother's company, as to our knowledge their minds aren't conditioned for a rebellion, a *'respondent conditioning'*[7], they're easier for us to read as they are 'operantly conditioned'[7], allowing our minds to feel superior to them. They give us a gift of pure love just by being in their presence as they love without a condition, you could probably egoically debate this as an animal can sometimes play out as if they only love you when you feed them, but that's more or less manifested in your mind, as a sense of you feeling superiorly needed, but you could debate this in your egoic conditioned mind for decades.

Truly look into an animal's eyes, or another human's eyes or go into nature without a technology device, you'll soon find your connection back to source. Back to the unconditional love, that the universe holds for you. As an example; It's so easy to watch a film and see how a female gets her heart broken by a male and gets her revenge or vice versa, causing the other pain, having an idea, a notion inside that love comes from the negative force, the pleasure and pain cycle evolving and love being the saviour to all your situations, as we are all connected by it. We are all made from it. We all go back to it. We are all searching for it. Why not show love to yourself today, know what your mind labels as your 'weakness' or your 'strengths', know what will help you and turn them into situations that will help you.

If you can't alchemise your own energy and situations, how are you supposed to thrive? How are you supposed to connect with others for what your soul craves? Why expect others to 'save' you when you don't know what will 'save' yourself? In these questions you will awaken your heart, sure they may be perceived as harsh to your mind, but you'll eventually realise it was your greatest strength all along.

The world needs people to rise with vulnerable hearts, that 'people' as a generalised term- is you.

The universe is calling you to rise.

To vibrate your essence through your heart space.

Be vulnerable.

Be clear about your vulnerability.

This, you will discover, is your greatest strength.

VII.   The Emotional Landscape.

Your emotions are merely energy in motion. All around you, you can see it, you can feel it, you know it's there. It's the cryptic codes in the stillness that we identify as air. It's the audience simultaneously crying at the movies, it's the giggles in a baby's happiness, it's the echoes of your cries into your pillow in your bedroom, it's the angst and insecurity in a retail shop, the frustration of a 'baby boomer' in front of a computer screen.

You have three eyes, two ears and one mouth, you see more than you hear, and you hear more than you speak. You only need to observe people and you'll realise the energy flooding out of them into the thin air. The vibrations they set off, they make you feel something, creating the awareness of trusting in your gut feeling.

As an example when asking an individual if they're okay and they tell you they're fine, their conditioned mind not responding to their own subconscious vibration they've manifested to make them aware of it. You responded. They reverted back to their safety, where they dis-identify with their energy in motion, they store it away for another time. They then build up an attraction for energies of this same type without even realising and they soon have an unknown energy field of emotions where they subconsciously attract similar energies to awaken their consciousness to recognise the energies going on in their 'being'. You, well you did your part and realised it didn't vibrate with the energy you were laying out in the universe. Your empathic nature picked it up and asked if this 'being' was aware of this emotion, they then consciously suppressed this emotion further. Inturn they have attached this energy into their subconscious mind of a triggered response and hence into their biological make-up. You've realised, you can't save them, they consciously don't want your help to awaken to their energy. There's nothing more you can do. Your conditioned mind makes it out as if there is a lot more that you can do.

In reflection, this is where your trap is in trying to awaken someone else. You can only lead by example, by showing them the difference between your energies and unconditional love towards it, not blaming them superiorly or reacting inferiorly with a victim story; it is there to empower you to acknowledging your own force. Within this force you realise how to accept and gracefully let go of an energy not serving your idea of your 'being'. Going around from situation to situation, holding onto a previous emotional response (energy), playing the blaming or victim game only creates more havoc, playing more games, it's not serving your soul as it's not vibrating in your heart space of unconditional love.

You are the universe having a human experience, you are love in the purest form, you will love and in this love, you are loved. You have the power to transform what you attract by transforming yourself first. You are whole all by yourself as you are at one with your mind, body and soul on this earth, consciously at this exact time frame.

This world is your landscape.

There are lessons from the energy everywhere, all around, passages, hills, oceans roaring, all to assist you in your human experience of evolutionising your soul. You attract what you need for your evolution, so you can reach a state where you attract what your soul wants. There's no greater lesson than these.

The overall world holds the power to manifest situations of conflict and peace in order for humans to develop in a collective consciousness. I'm sure with the ever-growing belief in spiritualism, that there will be a war over it through the mind conditioning identifying with a spiritual ego. Let's hope not. But this is the yin and yang, the imbalance of energies that creates conflict with individuals. The conflict starts from within you, where you begin to suppress the emotions, the energy in motion, that demands to be expressed and transmuted. This is where it begins and starts to attach to your being and identifying with your being instead of allowing it to run through you; you could blame it on a lot of events; for example, if you were silenced in school or by someone for speaking your truth. But ultimately in the present moment, it is up to you. It is up to you to change yourself, this is the power you hold. You can't blame others for the inability to understand your emotions, this is your time to learn about yourself, to behold the secrets to your own universe within yourself. Picture your body as the world (the landscape) and begin to encapture all the different energies running through, the places within that carry the positivity back through your being. The places that hold a negative vibration within, that can be triggered to erupt at any moment and encapsulate the feelings, where they come from, what they bring to you. Now, allow them to pass through you and escape, filling your being with the love you have hidden in the places, that you may have been unaware of.

This is your power, to encapsulate the divine unconditional love present from the source, this source being also inside you. This source is not something you search for externally, it's already within you that enables you to feel a sense of wholeness with the world and oneness with each being living presently. The world in which you find yourself is the reflection of your inner world. The world is your landscape for your emotions, it is created by your subconscious mind, to enable you to rise up to your power, become an awakened light for yourself and hence spread your light to the world. Without a connection to yourself you are in lack of connecting adequately to your outer world.

Also, on the other hand, if you lack a connection with the world, you've lacked a connection to your divine soul's mission. There's a reason you are here, there's a reason you've encountered the experiences you have, and that reason, my darling reader, is you.

Your own being has subconsciously manifested your own experiences to this day and beyond, in order for your soul to develop and benefit the collective consciousness and vibration of the world. As all is energy, you rise, he rises, she rises; you fall, he falls, she falls. Although every experience has a lesson you rise for lessons, you fall for lessons. You've manifested these experiences, for lessons, willingly or unwillingly, nothing is merely in your control, as it's all due to a divine plan. You've made choices based on your feelings (emotions and energy) you've made these on a subconscious level to awaken to your own divine purpose. These experiences have merely unfolded before you, these emotions, energy in motion, merely triggered inside you, to enable your conscious mind to become aware of what is required to heal your inner self.

Ignoring these emotions or needs for healing, towards a 'band-aid effect' or suppression, only pushes down this emotion, this energy, to store inside your body, until your subconscious manifests another event alike it, maybe more intense this time, to again awaken you to this need for healing. Some individual beings will go on a repeated loop of this, their whole existence in the three-dimensional realm, and bring it with their energy force even into the next realm. Some individuals will awaken and realise the necessity for their healing to be underway. They feel the calling, they know it's here, they knew they need a change they just consciously are unsure of what. They're ready for the next stage of their soul's growth, to come back into their alignment with their higher self and the universe and nature. They come back into alignment with the fifth dimension that one is unable to describe, but they feel a sense of love and wholeness, this is the Universe, God. They come back into alignment with their feelings of interpretation in their being, their fourth dimensional being state. Further they come back to the connection of the three dimensional God-like, Universal source itself, nature, humans, animals, those connections of oneness with the hearts of the collective in the world.

This is your power. This is your alignment. This is what you behold inside you, when you begin to encapsulate the essence of your potential. This is your connection with your soul purpose, the connection of the law of attraction, the connection of raising your vibrational frequency, healing your inner child, energetic aura.

This is your power.

This is all within you and once it's reflected without you, you've grasped the emotional landscape. The energy that is existentially ready to provide you with the nature and necessities to help light the way, with all those before you and all those after you. You are reflecting the light that is within your own being, onto the light of the universe, complimenting the scenery. The energy within you that is not serving your divine purpose will begin to show, as you will manifest these situations in your outer world. These events will occur, the only difference is, you're awake and begin to realise it wasn't the experience that was the issue all along, it wasn't merely the energy set off either. You begin to realise the force that your life has with your outer world. You begin to observe and watch the energy run through your body into the outer space, embracing the emptiness inside once you have observed this.

You begin to realise what you are left with, this being you.

The stillness.

Nothing more and nothing less.

You can then allow your being to flood with a relief of embracing the energy that moved through and fill your being with the love from the divine source inside you. The unconditional love, that you've allowed the event to pass through you, without making your body into a cemetery for emotions. You fall back on the love of the divine. You fall back on the unconditional trust and love. You then gain the lesson from the event that your 'being' manifested and encountered. The lesson may need to be alchemised to turn the negative to a positive to instill your heart with the positive energetic vibration of the experience. Some will capture this through journaling, meditating, creating a picture, craft, business, essay, art, music, any creation to enable that energetic flow to be awarded through the being and projected into the world. This is how your soul develops your emotional landscape, without possibly your 'being' knowingly being aware of this. Through creations you can tap into your right-brain hemisphere, the feminine side to your energetic field and embrace your lessons and express your emotions, the energy in motion, into the world, to benefit the collective consciousness.

This is the power your being holds, you hold. Awaken to your ever-growing potential, as it is your ever-growing soul's evolution. Whether you're reading this enclosed in a three-dimensional mindset, fourth-dimensional or fifth-dimensional mindset, this is to awaken you to realign to your soul's mission. You came here to rise. You came here to learn, this outer world is a projection of your inner world. This outer world can be compared to a school in the three dimensional world, where the world is your learning ground. Your events are not merely events without a purpose, a purpose for you to unlock the lesson within yourself. Fall back on love for all in the outer world and you will fall back on love for all in your inner world. There is no greater power than the power of love.

VIII. The Polarity of Balancing Energies.

The polarity of balancing the divine masculine energy and the divine feminine energy is the key to unlocking your soul's mission. Once you have balanced your masculine and feminine energies inside, you will have the awareness of the adequate emotional landscape. Once you've grasped the divine of the two energies inside you, you begin to surpass the conditioning of the society as a whole collective, hence unlocking the ever-growing, ever-blossoming potential of your three-dimensional, fourth-dimensional and fifth-dimensional self. Let me explain to you why.

The left-side of our brain encompasses our logical, three-dimensional needed side, whilst the right side of our brain grasps the necessities for your creative side, the fifth-dimensional self. Through the left you begin to have the divine masculine side, that enables the self to survive in the third-dimensional reality through reasoning and logic.

The right-side of the brain, the divine feminine side, channels the creative, rhythmic, vibrational flow of the universal force. Unlocking your mind and becoming aware of your own inner world, allows you to categorise your outer world into the conditioning of your inner child.

Further embracing your world and awakening to the endless possibilities of the universal force, you can encompass the healing for your inner child through the expression of creativity. Realising that in essence this is the flow of your natural being inside, you begin to see this depicted in your outside world through similarities of events and experiences. Once you've reached the state of awareness, your logical mind begins to have a reasoning mindset and begins to grow. If you unlock this within your whole self you encompass the growth mindset of the fourth-dimensional reality, whereby you unveil the law of attraction, laws of vibrations, where you can realise the empowerment that your being has on your own soul's evolution, in the present moment. Balancing out the necessary nature of the masculine energy and feminine energy, as you begin to see and become aware of the existential truth of why you have a necessary mission to be present in the third-dimension of the matriarchal system of a dominant masculine built energy, of logic and reasoning and why your being is also required in connection with the fifth-dimensional, creative, feminine energy, as you see the necessity for bringing unconditional love, from the feeling of oneness and wholeness with the universe, down to the constructed matrix system.

Looking beyond how the conditioned mind labels the feminine and masculine energies, your being in the third-dimension, as your physical body, it's much more than what genitalia your physical body is identified with. This is the energy, the life force, of male and female in all of us, each one of us is created from it and will create with it. It's embedded in our three-dimensional body, we are made of masculine and feminine energy. Every choice you've ever made has encountered your intuition, creative side, feminine side, and your logical, reasoning side, masculine side. There's no 'right' nor 'wrong', no debates needed, it's an existential truth.

You are connected to each being, whether masculine or feminine, in all realms. You are connected with all source, masculine or feminine in all realms, the same way you are connected to the oneness feeling, the feeling of wholeness. Once you are conditioned within your mind, reacting on your operant or 'respondent conditioning'[7], you are allowing the energies, the emotions to build up inside you, keeping these emotions inside as triggers. Don't allow yourself to become a slave to the conditioning, to the ever-growing circle of the physical, three-dimensional, matriarchal, matrix realm, of categorising your being into a thought-up concept, in order to accustom yourself to the thought-up concept of the three-dimensional realm.

Admittedly involuntarily or voluntarily proceeding to escape your conditioned mind to reason or logic of the system, through the masculine energy of paradoxically labelling yourself into a three-dimensional concept... to escape your three-dimensional mind. Reverting back to 'respondent conditioning'[7] of the opposite, feminine energy, to the extreme masculine energy, to which you'll discover both a complete made-up concept of the matriarchal society as a whole.

Your body is not your be all and end all, your mind is not your be all and end all, they are both merely tools to use in your soul's mission to raise the collective consciousness. Once you've given recognition to each, you can rise to understand the impacts of the unconditional love of the universe, to embrace your emotional landscape. You are just a being, having a human experience. There is a masculine and feminine energy in each individual, to which requires a balancing out of these two, to embrace your soul's purpose.

You'll find eventually that you revert back to love and embrace the need to lead by example. You uncover more than your body, more than your mind, more than just a judgement on what you perceive and begin to encounter the truth of your connection and oneness with the world and the universe.

As a brief example: The feminist movement today has women, acting as men to beat the man in a 'man's world', and the men acting in their feminine side to survive in the 'women's world'. The irony of this is that the truth is to thrive we must come back to our equilibrium, our balance of the unconditional love and acceptance of the other being, despite our three-dimensional physical body or conditioned mind-sets. Taking control of our beings, reflecting on our actions, reflecting on the events raised by our own subconscious to understand what we need healed inside. There will be no need to feel an inadequacy when we balance out our inner worlds, and heal our own inner child trauma. We will see the balance in our outside worlds, as it will reflect back to you. Your outer world is your inner world and inner world is your outer world. You attract the energy and situations you need in order to identify where to balance out your energies, as some triggers inside you will allow your mind to acknowledge your physical body's innate reaction to the circumstance. Allowing you to realise where the energy doesn't run all the way through you and back into the universe, but stays in your body, keeping your conditioned mind on an infinite loop of why your physical body responded the way it did, articulated itself the way it did. Your feminine energy comes in to override your mind, towards the universal flow of your soul evolutionary purpose, if you allow your mind to recognise it and embrace the construction of uncertainty and then trust. All of this is the tools your mind creates for your evolutionary purpose subconsciously, hence universally consciously. Always having a plan, to fall back on the power within you, but is cryptic to your three-dimensional self. This is the universal order of evolution.

The balancing of the divine masculine and feminine energies can assist in your evolution through escaping the in-built need to judge, analyse and over-exasperate, your physical three-dimensional being. You can begin to appreciate yourself for all you are and all you have to give in this world, without suppressing the needs of your unconscious desires to ostracise yourself and others, in order to attempt to fit into the matriarchal three-dimensional system. The same system that raised you to be who you are right now, can only destroy you if you subconsciously destroy yourself. Once you heal yourself, you have the power to heal the world. Once you rise in your own vibration, you rise for the whole collective vibration. It's just the existential truth of the universe.

There's positives and negatives to each energy, (formulated on the basis of your own conditioned mind view point), although even the notion of positivity and negativity is only a concept, an idea, as you can alchemise your negativity into positivity, through learning the lessons that enable your soul to grow. Each energy is merely an energy that can be alchemised either way.

An example is the masculine energy; As you may find the masculine energy egoic in its nature, the alchemy of this is: The ego is an essential tool to survive in the physical three-dimensional realm, to some extent. The masculine energy, provides also a yearning for searching and developing your ever-growing need to evolutionise when relating to your knowledge, due to the subconscious need for reasoning and logic. When alchemising this need (as seen in the example) it is a helpful energy, as you can relate it to each event and experience in your 'reality', through finding how this event is relatable to your inner being and how it is helping your evolutionary purpose. This provides the basis of how the masculine energy is essential in your evolution.

Balancing these notions (of each of the two energies into one energy this being, you) you fall back on the feminine energy inside, to relate it to a higher self and the universe. The feminine energy allows a nurturing feeling of love, that entails the limitless opportunities of the universe. Bringing this energy into your masculine conditioned mind enables you to go beyond the realm of the third-dimension, into a fourth-dimension of growth, where you embody the limitless universal potential, into your third-dimensional self. Taking a loving approach into your physical being of the third-dimension, hence into your mind-set of the fourth-dimension to nourish your inner world to positively influence your outer world. This is how your divine masculine and divine feminine energies work together. Inside yourself and hence reflecting on your outside world, as once you heal your energies into alignment, you will have an awareness of this balance and gravitate towards others in this balance, as once you give this intertwining recognition on the inside, you can further embrace the intertwining on your outside world, through a sense of wholeness within yourself. Although if you are out of balance with an energy inside of you, you will attract this energy towards you to compensate for your mind thinking you are lacking in that energy, and gravitate towards the yearning of feeling at a lack and needing another or a collective to fulfil it.

You can further embrace the balance within, through a sense of oneness and connectivity, as you embrace them with a sense of oneness and connectivity and hence embracing the notion of the universal unconditional love. You can accept other beings for the energy they allow you to feel and radiate that energy further in communion with the other person's company. Where the only logic you can place to articulate it is, pure love, this sense of coming back to a resemblance of a home type feeling. The connection of the infinite balance of the divine, the peace and harmony that exuberates your emotional landscape. The feeling of knowing you are connected and loved. This is the balance of the two polarities of nature and the universe, masculine and feminine, three-dimensional and fifth-dimensional, created in your inner world and reflected in your outer world.

IX.   The Return to the Unconditional.

The returning to the universal flow. The return requires a limitless belief that love is all around. This is the universe. There is unconditional love in any motive when alchemised appropriately. If you fall back on love, you will realise why you went through the events that you have, and why you'll go through the events that you have, and why you'll go through the events you will go through in the future. All the experiences you encounter are designed by your own being to show you a part of you that needs healing, what greater love for your 'being' is there, than this. Those blame games your mind tends to play about how someone did something to you, they played that role in your life to show you the parts of you that needed to develop. Those individual people your mind extrapolates to, 'they were the issue', 'it's their fault', gives you an opportunity to grow, to fall back on the universal flow of unconditional love, they loved you that much they came in your life to show you a part of yourself that needed healing, what greater love is there than this? Those victim stories your mind holds onto to clench on and develop an egoic conditioning of what you pride yourself subconsciously on. You've stored those energetic, emotional bodies inside your physical body and further your subconscious mind your whole life. When your subconscious manifests an event to uncover the need for healing, you react on that trigger (from the energetic, emotional body) rather than releasing the emotion. This is the reasoning of the repetition of your soul's evolution.

You react on the trigger, rather than releasing the emotion to run through you, and learning the lessons of the event. You blame the characters, the scenery, victimising the characters, forgetting about the existential truth. That character played the role in your life to awaken your healing. That character played just the role, in this life that's all they were, just a role to awaken you to your own potential. They awaken the love inside you, for the universe. This love encompasses your being, and connection with other beings and the universe. The unconditional love that is inside and around us all, waiting to come through you to shine its truth.

To balance the yin and yang of the world, the divine masculine and feminine energies inside, will help embody the collective consciousness to a new form of awareness. It's the lessons and disasters, it's the appeared love and unloveable, it is inside every single molecule build-up in every realm. It's the potential that even when you scream that you have given up, that the universal force of unconditional love will save you from anything. Any event you find yourself in. It's knowing that despite anything you have been through there's a force of the unconditional love that upholds everything. It is here to assist you and fill you with anything, you deem you require clarity on. That is returning to the unconditional. That despite it all, and despite anything it will fill you with peace and belief. Despite anything and everything that your mind manifests you to heal; know you are loved, because you are made of love. There is love all around and there is no need to search further than within yourself.

Glossary

Alchemy: Having a connection with the universe, soul purpose and others by showing gratitude towards a negative situation, in order to gain a positive outcome. Transmuting energy.

Alignment: Coming into the same vibrational alignment (energy force) of your soul.

Authenticity: Being true to yourself. Showing your soul nature. Your natural self.

Behaviourist: Someone attaining a degree in the study of how human's behave overall.

Capitalism: Privately owned industries.

Conscious: Your awareness of your current mindset of everyday.

Condition: The outcome of nurturing something. i.e. the conditioning of your mind at this time has resulted from nurture in some form.

Corporations: Industries.

Channeling: Connection with your higher self (soul) hence with the divine (universe/god).

Evolution: Growth from your life experiences.

Existential: Universe.

Empath: The ability to understand a situation from all different points of views; from the energetic frequency.

Existential truth: Your higher purpose truth, soul, universal purpose.

Feminine-energy: I relate this to our identity of the right side of the brain-creativity, conscious thinking, unconditionally loving, connecting.

Hierarchical order: In relation to the sense of a hierarchy when referring to society.

Higher purpose/ soul mission: Your life purpose, why you are here consciously at this exact moment in time.

Imperialism: Policies that enables countries to have power through rights of land by using their created powers of the law, army, currency.

Information: Knowledge.

Inferior: Feeling less than something or someone.

Innate: The natural condition of someone or something from birth (survival skills).

Mindset: Current state of how you view your life.

Materialism: Material state of awareness, relying on objects to serve a state of happiness.

Matrix: The hierarchy of the corporate world from the conditioned human minds.

Matriarchy: The hierarchy of the corporate world from the conditioned human minds.

Manifest: Bringing something into your conscious awareness.

Masculine-energy: I relate this to our identity of the left side of the brain- logic, reasoning, ego-driven, having proof.

Narcissist: The notion of being ego-driven, not in your heart space of unconditional love.

New World Order: The evolution of the third-dimension.

Programmed: Being fed information and believing it all, so you don't question your life and merely become a television program- repeating information you've been led to believe.

Paradigm: Showing something side-by-side.

Paradox: Something you have been led to believe as true, yet it contradicts itself in a logical sense.

Psychologist: Someone attaining a degree in the study of the mind.

Reptilian brain: Our survival mind, natural state of the egoic mind.

Soul: spirit; Eg. When you close your eyes and open them, whilst having your eyes closed, you can see the back of your eyelids- the eyes are the portal to the soul-literally the energy grounded inside your physical body.

System: Construct.

Society: Generalisation of the human species into a collective.

Societal structure: How society is structured in what people call 'reality'.

Superior: Feeling more than something or someone.

Subconscious: The subconscious state of mind that stores the information to bring it to the conscious state of mind when it is needed.

Unconscious: The notion of not being aware of your mind in particular conscious thinking.

Unconditional love: The notion of loving with no conditions, such as expectations or ideals.

Vibration: Energy.

Vulnerable: The feeling of insecurity in opening your heart in a situation.

Yin-Yang: The positive energy and negative energy, balancing each other out in unison.

Bibliography: Reference List:

Austrian, G.D. (1982). *Forgotten Giant of Information Processing*. USA: Columbia University Press.

Bhalla, S. (1920). *Quotes of Gandhi*. U B S Publishers' Distributors Ltd.

Bowlby, J. (1982). *Attachment and Loss Volume I Second Edition*. London: The Hogarth Press and The Institute of Psycho-Analysis.

Caddy, E. (1988). *Flight into Freedom The Autobiography of the Co-founder of the Findhorn Community*. Element Books Ltd.

Jung, G.C. (1958). *The Collected Works of C.G.Jung: Psychology and Religion, volume II*. England, London: Routledge & Kegan Paul L.T.D.

Kerrigan, M. (2003). *Shakespeare on Love*. Penguin Books Australia.

Lama, D. (1995). *His Holiness The Dalai Lama Awakening the Mind Lightening the Heart*. The Liberty of Tibet.

Maslow, A.H. (1968). *Toward A Psychology of Being. Second Edition*. United States of America: Van Nostrand Reinhold Company.

Morgan Arts Council (2018, January 24). *Gregg Braden 2018 – Human by Design* [Youtube]. Retrieved from https://www.youtube.com/watch?v=7C_8q46WyEg.

Packard, V. (1961). *The Status Seekers: An Explosive Exploration of Class Behavior in America and The Hidden Barriers That Affect You, Your Community and Your Future*. Giant Cardinal.

Piaget, J. (1953). *The Origin of Intelligence in the Child*. London, England: Routledge & Kegan Paul.

Rhodes, F.H.T. (1962). *The Evolution of Life*. Cox and Wyman Ltd.

Skinner, B.F. (1974). *About Behaviourism.* Great Britain: Jonathan Cape.

Tolbert, E.L. (1959). *Introduction to Conseling.* McGraw-Hill Book Company, INC.

Tolle, E. (2004), p.36. *The Power of Now.* Australia and New Zealand: Hodder Australia.

10813417R00044

Printed in Great Britain
by Amazon